HAUS CURIOSITIES

*The Kingdom to Come*

D1386612

For Cecily, Mick, Joe and Jack Cromby
*My family in Scotland*

## About the Author

Peter Hennessy was educated at Marling School, Stroud; St John's College, Cambridge; the London School of Economics; and Harvard, where he was a Kennedy Scholar 1971–72. He spent 20 years in journalism with spells on *The Times*, the *Financial Times* and *The Economist* and as a presenter of the BBC Radio 4 *Analysis* programme. He is a Fellow of the British Academy and sits as an independent crossbench peer in the House of Lords as Lord Hennessy of Nympsfield. He is Attlee Professor of Contemporary British History at Queen Mary, University of London.

Peter Hennessy

# THE KINGDOM TO COME

*Thoughts on the Union before and
after the Scottish referendum*

**HAUS
CURIOSITIES**

First published by Haus Publishing in 2015
70 Cadogan Place
London SW1X 9AH
*www.hauspublishing.com*

A CIP catalogue record for this book is
available from the British Library

Print ISBN: 978-1-910376-06-5
Ebook ISBN: 978-1-910376-23-2

Typeset in Garamond by MacGuru Ltd
*info@macguru.org.uk*

Printed in Spain

# Preface: A Union Man

'The stakes are very high. And, of course, after the drama of the Scottish referendum, we have to worry about the UK. We have to worry about what we need to do so that we don't have such a scare ever again, where 45 per cent of the people in a major constituent part of the UK vote to leave it.'

William Hague, First Secretary of State and Leader of the House of Commons, speaking on *The Kingdom to Come*, BBC Radio 4, 19 December 2014

'In Scotland after the referendum many felt great disappointment, while others felt great relief, and bridging these differences will take time'.

'Her Majesty's Address to the Nation and the Commonwealth', BBC 1, Christmas Day, 25 December 2014

A degree of detachment is – or should be – part of a historian's mentalité. This is quite stretching for any observer of his or her own country when writing about a period through which one has lived, especially if it's a treatment of very recent events.

I cannot in this instance even mount a pretence of detachment. For when it comes to the United Kingdom, I am a

Union man. For me the Union is a matter as much of emotional geography as it is political or physical. I have always lived and breathed as a Brit, imagined as a Brit, rejoiced as a Brit or, on rare occasions, despaired of my country's fortunes as a Brit. Had Scotland separated in 2014, for me it would have been like a bereavement; for what would have become 'the Remainder of the UK' it would have been an impoverishment in almost every sense.

That it did not happen remains for me a cause of immense relief – but it is a relief tinged with a continuing anxiety. The Union, I fear, is far from steady six months after the referendum.

The reasons for my being a convinced unionist will, I hope, emerge in the pages that follow, especially in thoughts recalling formative years as a child of the early post-war era. Fearing for the Union came quite late in life. For I was among those who thought that the devolution of powers to Scotland in the Scotland Act of 1998 and the creation of a new Scottish Parliament in 1999 would draw the sting out of Scottish nationalism and preserve the Union at least for the duration of my lifetime. Historians can make rotten forecasters.

Contemporary historians, too, can be tempted to airbrush out the moments when their first draft of a breaking story went wonky, whether through under-reaction, over-reaction or simple miscomprehension. So part of this pamphlet is a diary I kept from July 2014 to just after the mid-September referendum, recording how I thought and felt about developments and prospects at a particular moment.

The diary is used in Part One to convey how the result struck me at the time, before I turn to thoughts firstly on the immediate aftermath and then about what the country was facing in the Spring of 2015 in politico-constitutional terms, as the General Election campaign threw out its peculiar mixture of great heat and rather less light. Part Two is entirely diary. The pamphlet starts, however, with a brief touch on Scotland's Northern Isles in the summer of 1914, when the UK faced a threat from without rather than from within, exactly a century before I picked up my pen to start drafting *The Kingdom to Come*.

Peter Hennessy
*South Ronaldsay, Walthamstow, Westminster and Sheffield*
*February 2015*

# Contents

# Introduction: Thoughts from South Ronaldsay: Hope, anxiety and the shadow of Orwell

I am writing these opening words overlooking Scapa Flow and surrounded by the gentle rim of the Orkney Islands in the last days of July 2014. Exactly a century ago Winston Churchill, as First Lord of the Admiralty, despatched swiftly and secretly what was to become the Royal Navy's Grand Fleet from its Dorset base in Portland to its forward base for a Great Power War, in the waters of this huge natural harbour north of the turbulent Pentland Firth where the North Sea meets the Atlantic.

In his vivid account in *The World Crisis 1911–1915*, first published in 1923, Churchill allied a brilliant imagination to a pen as punchy as any Dreadnought:

> We may now picture this great Fleet, with its flotillas and cruisers, steaming slowly out of Portland Harbour, squadron by squadron, scores of gigantic castles of steel wending their way across the misty shining sea, like giants bowed in anxious thought ...
>
> If war should come no one would know where to look for the British Fleet. Somewhere in that enormous waste of waters to the north of our islands ... shrouded in storms and mists, dwelt this mighty organization.[1]

A hundred years ago the waters before me became the geopolitical centre of the world. From here the mightiest seaborne force the world had ever seen would operate what was confidently, though erroneously, expected to be a war-shortening economic blockade against Imperial Germany. From here the King's Dreadnoughts and battle cruisers would sail if there was to be, as was also expected, a great day of reckoning with the Kaiser's High Seas Fleet, steaming out with their accompanying flotillas of escorts through the narrow Hoxa Sound between the islands of South Ronaldsay and Flotta – as they later did in May 1916, on their way to the Battle of Jutland off Denmark.

The serene waters in front of me this calm summer morning inspire hope. No visitor to Orkney would, unless well primed, have any sense of this place's significance in both the great conflicts of the twentieth century, at least until their cars and coaches took them past old gun emplacements at the entrances to the Flow or carried them across the Churchill Barriers, thrown up in haste after a U-boat crept in and sank the *Royal Oak* in the opening weeks of World War II. In the depths, too, are thousands of tons of finest Kaiser-commissioned steel, deposited there in June 1919 by a German Admiral ordering a Grand Scuttle of the incarcerated High Seas Fleet.

For all the calm, the blissful sense of temporary escape, there lurks in my mind a sense of anxiety mingled with hope, as we are less than two months away from a referendum on Scottish Independence which could rupture the United Kingdom I've called home since my first conscious memories at the turn of the 1940s and 1950s. The referendum could alter its very configuration for ever.

In no way could any Brit on Armistice Day 1918 have foreseen the circumstances in which the Union of 1707 might be reversed. The preoccupation then was Ireland. The foundation of the Scottish National Party – through a merger of the National Party of Scotland and the Scottish Party – was 15 years in the future.

My own individual sense of Scotland began to form in the 1950s. Napoleon liked to remark that if you wished to understand a man or woman, you needed to appreciate the world as it was when they were 20.[2] In my case it's earlier than that. It's between the ages of six and ten – Coronation Year 1953 and my first visit to Scotland in 1957.

It's hard to recapture the moods and mentalities of early post-war Britain or even the party system in which they were played out, despite the main political groupings carrying much the same labels as they do today, though the Tories were firmly known as the Conservative and Unionist Party and the Liberals had yet to acquire the word 'Democrat'. There was no equivalent of the United Kingdom Independence Party, though there was, on the rightist fringe, the League of Empire Loyalists, who wanted to remain territorially intimate with large parts of the world rather than wishing, like UKIP, for the opposite.

Family conversations often began in those days with either 'before the war', 'during the war', or 'after the war'. The Second World War was the pivot, *the* shared experience above all others, the creator of the emotional geography of the nation and its politics – and that nation was very definitely a united kingdom. We had stood firm alone on our own after the fall of France in June 1940 until Hitler's invasion of Russia in June 1941. With our allies, we had eventually prevailed in 1945 as *Brits*. It was the last time we acted powerfully and collectively together as a union over a sustained period. The fleeting moments we have done so since – the Coronation of Queen Elizabeth in 1953; the Falklands War of 1982; the London Olympics of 2012 – have served, particularly over the last 30 years, only to emphasise the leaching away of the sentiments derived from shared experiences over the decades since 1939–45.

One mustn't overdo what that remarkable social historian, Peter Laslett, called 'The World We Have Lost'.[3] Though we may not always feel it, there is much more of that early post-war world that runs through to today than one might think. It is not a matter of the occasional faint pulsar getting through from a long-faded political, economic and social solar system. The National Health Service remains the emblem of that era – of institutionalised altruism, pooled risk and a level of social solidarity. Right from the start, in July 1948, it has been a bond and a talisman of shared citizenship, with its services taxpayer-funded and free at the point of delivery. And the NHS was a UK-wide phenomenon. Its bonding effect was just as powerful in Scotland as it was in England. Above all, it was a *national* service regionally and locally administered.

The first decade after the war saw another form of all-in-it-togetherness – male bonding in this case; military conscription or National Service, as we called it. Clem Attlee once told his Cabinet that National Service was the way young British males could give something back in return for the new welfare state.[4]

Public ownership, another brand of the Labour government's 1945–51 programme, was called by its protagonists such as Herbert Morrison the 'Socialization of Industry', which never caught on as a label. It was universally known as nationalisation – the new publicly owned industries were overseen by a National Coal Board or a British Transport Commission running British Railways. We still thought nationally – and national meant UK national. Today that really is, the NHS apart, a distant, departed world. And even in the case of the Health Service we agonise perpetually about the balance of public and private provision.

The great rush of post-1945 institution-building owed much to the wartime experience of a thoroughly mobilised home front centrally overseen. A second key factor was the blueprint provided by the Beveridge Report of 1942, whose central thesis was that unless the elements of deprivation – the 'Five Giants on the Road to Reconstruction' (Ignorance, Idleness, Disease, Squalor, Want) – were struck simultaneously, their tough outer crust would not crack.[5] The Beveridge prescriptions, which shaped the first post-war decades, made us think in national terms too.

Thinking UK, imagining nationally, was so natural that we believed it was the norm – if we thought about it at all. Most of the time we didn't. We knew who we were and did not need to define it or fret over it. The same was true of continuing to cut a dash in the world as a great power, something we *did* think rather more about, not least because it cost close to 10 per cent of our national wealth in defence spending and because there were some humiliating setbacks, the Suez Affair of 1956 in particular.

1953, Coronation Year, still glows in my memory as a great national event that somehow brought all our national ingredients together, all our constituent elements – not just the 'home nations', as we called England, Scotland, Wales and Northern Ireland, but the extended family (as we still conceived it) living in dominion, colony and protectorate. All this *and* a Commonwealth expedition putting the first men on top of Everest, a New Zealander and a Sherpa, in time for the news to reach London on a damp but still dazzling Coronation morning. We were naturals when it came to blending tradition (the superb Coronation ceremony) and modernity (the first jet civil airliner, the Comet, and soon, at Cumberland's Calder Hall, the first civil nuclear power station to feed into a national grid).

So much for wider formative impulses. The Scottish element had to wait until June 1957 when my parents, my sister Maureen and I set off from Finchley in the North London suburbs in a hired Ford Prefect laden with camping equipment for the Isle of Skye, though the family rang to stories of Mum and Dad climbing in the Cuillins of Skye and elsewhere before the war. The journey up the east side of England then Scotland took, I think, 2½ days. My first sight of Scotland? Crossing Carter Bar and into the Southern Uplands. Soon it was Edinburgh, on the Parks side, late evening and down to Queensferry to catch the last boat to Fife beneath the Forth Rail Bridge (no road bridge then), which lived up to its fabled billing silhouetted against the twilight of a Scottish mid-summer evening. Powerful stuff with more to come – consuming my first ever Scotch pancake in Inverness, the road from Dingwall west amazingly narrow for an 'A' road to a London boy's eyes (an 'A' road with passing places?). Crossing the Strome Ferry then the dramatic pier head at Kyle of Lochalsh, the ferry to Kyleakin and Skye, turning left at Broadford for a rented house overlooking the Sound of Sleat.

Skye itself was a magic isle. The black gabbro of the Cuillin skyline (too young to climb to the ridge). Dunvegan Castle. Journey back via Fort Augustus. Nearly eaten alive by the early-summer midges while camping overnight at Crianlarich – an incentive to a very early start, crossing the Erskine Ferry carrying a sizeable workforce to the morning shifts over a Clyde bedecked with shipyards, before lunch with relations near Kilmarnock. The contrast between the last thrust of the Highlands down Loch Lomond and the heaving industrial central belt bit into my boyish memory as deeply as the water and the mountains already had. From then on, to parody the opening sentence of Charles de Gaulle's memoirs about France,[6] I always had a certain idea of Scotland.

Countless visits since 1957, as a journalist, historian, holidaymaker, parent and grandparent to the family in Orkney, have added to this vivid first impression of a special land that was part of my certain idea of Britain back in 1957.

The years between 1957 and 2014 have given me a harder-edged appreciation of the specialness of Scotland. I was, for example, a tad untutored about the Scottish Enlightenment in the mid-Fifties though I had a sense of Scottish genius where iron and steel met slipway or railway bridge. Add in the disproportionate contribution from a country of 5 million to the other 55m in the UK in terms of military and public service in various forms, university teaching and research, finance and UK political life and you have what should be one of the most self-confident nations on earth – a true exemplar to countries large as well as small.

However, to an outside eavesdropper on Scotland's domestic political conversation in the run-up to the referendum, the worst of the cyber-trolling and some of the speeches hint at a stridency and a narrowness that suggest a malign blend of insecurity, resentment and a profound lack of generosity of spirit towards opponents.

My own British patriotism is powerful but understated, shaped by the shadow of George Orwell's classic wartime essay, *The Lion and the Unicorn*,[7] though I could never aspire to the mix of thought, feeling and vocabulary he brought to his task when he sat down at his home in North London during the late summer blitz of 1940 and wrote this opening sentence: 'As I write, highly civilized human beings are flying overhead, trying to kill me.'[8]

Orwell in *The Lion and the Unicorn* constantly refers to his country as 'England'. Indeed, the subtitle of his extended essay, first published in 1941, is 'Socialism and the English Genius'. My word is 'Britain' and, to adapt one of the best-known lines within Orwell's pages, I have often seen Britain as 'a family with the wrong members in control'.[9] And it is Orwell's sense of extended family – in July 2014, a UK extended family in jeopardy – that preoccupies me. I don't wish to find myself in less than two months' time on the way to living in what I shall always regard as my country, my turf – but now with a border between the Solway Firth and the mouth of the Tweed. I do not wish in the years to come, when I return from visiting the family in the Northern Isles, to have to overfly a foreign country for the first 400 miles of my journey back to London.

Pessimism is not my strongest suit. Quite the reverse. I possess perhaps excessive faith in the UK – that we will find a way through with our allies whatever we are up against, whether it be the Kaiser, Hitler or Stalin and his successors – or any 'ism', person or country likely to threaten our existence or the special cluster of characteristics and practices we bundle together inside our borders. If I were putting a subtitle beneath a 'Lion and the Unicorn' strapline it would be:

SMART MUDDLING THROUGH AND THE BRITISH GENIUS

This is a version of what the political theorist, David Runciman, calls 'the confidence trap'. Runciman suggests that mature and deep-set democracies like ours can have too much confidence in our adaptability – an adaptability that comes from being open societies prone to internal rows. This adaptability we believe will, in the end, and in a messy and often indeterminate way, always somehow see off the tyrannical, the authoritarian and the menacing.[10] I am prone in my rare moments of gloom, to agree with a wise friend of mine who spent his life inside the Secret Intelligence Service, attempting to thwart the Queen's adversaries overseas. He has long believed that the people we find hardest to defend against are ourselves. And some of our internal arguments on the road to the referendum of 2014 have turned into 'domestics' that threaten not just the peace of our everyday lives but our very existence as a united kingdom at home and as a thoroughly outward-looking nation abroad. Said 'domestics' go under the labels of the 'Scottish Question' and 'Britain in Europe'. One thing is sure: the shared experience of the Scottish

Question will not leave political relationships as they were nor the nature of the United Kingdom unchanged. The 2014 referendum will score a line across the history of these islands, even if it does not cut sufficiently deep to sever.

The day before I depart South Ronaldsay, *The Scotsman* publishes the names of 200 people the paper describes as 'celebrities and public figures' who have signed a letter organised by Tom Holland and Dan Snow that sings a song of union (I was among the choristers):

> The decision on whether to leave our shared country is, of course, absolutely yours alone. Nevertheless, we want to let you know how very much we value our bonds of citizenship with you. What unites us is much greater than what divides us. Let's stay together.[11]

Amen to that.

# Part one

# The result: the view from Westminster

It is difficult to write a diary when you are in a television studio. Here in diary form is the result as I recorded it the day after it was plain the kingdom was not to sunder.

## Saturday 20 September
### *Sheffield*
Travelled up here yesterday on the afternoon train for brother-in-law Douglas's 65th birthday dinner. Writing this late afternoon. Relief still coursing through the capillaries.

Final result:

| | |
|---|---|
| No: | 55.3%; Yes 44.7% |
| No: | 2,001,926 votes |
| Yes: | 1,617,989 votes |
| Turnout: | 84.59% |
| Male: | 53% No; 47% Yes |
| Female: | 56% No; 44% Yes[12] |

Phew.

Kingdom survives; HM Queen calls for unity; Salmond to stand down as First Minister in November.

Immediate political fallings out over whether or not the new powers promised for Scotland will materialise and how soon.

Managed to scribble down a few notes during the long night with the BBC 1 results programme; the early-morning appearance on *Today* and lunchtime with *The Daily Politics* on BBC 2 ...

**Thursday night/Friday morning 18–19 September 2014**
Arrived at 3 Albert Embankment just before 11pm. Millbank is being done up so the BBC took a studio five floors up with a stunning view across the river to the lit terrace of the Houses of Parliament and the MI5 HQ at Thames House as the backdrop.

Go up to the top of the building about 11.20pm to a makeshift radio studio to talk to Jim Naughtie in Glasgow, who's anchoring the Radio 4 results programme. Jim asks me about HMQ. I say any biography of her will now linger on the Crathie moment last Sunday, the photo of her about to chat to the well-wishers and how niftily and technically neutrally it was done. [The Queen had just asked the people of Scotland to think carefully before casting their vote. See page 110.] I added that one can't impute views to others – let alone the Sovereign – but it's known she loves every particle of her kingdom. We talk about the 1977 speech to both Houses of Parliament, when in her Jubilee year she reminded the country that she had been crowned 'Queen of the United Kingdom of Great Britain and Northern Ireland'.

Why is this so special? I say to Jim that he and I have both been round the block a bit – but we've known nothing like this. Not like any of the 40 independence settlements with portions of the former British Empire between 1947 and 1980. This is flesh of our flesh. If Scotland goes it won't be severance. It will be rending. No general election night compares. 'It really is different. It's about a kingdom.' I tell Jim that by first light we will be a different country whatever the result. The English Question up till now has been a growl; by breakfast time it will be starting to roar. It'll be a question of England Arise.

I'm pretty tense. Slightly jumpy. Can't relax to any degree.

Come back to the Green Room to join Kate Williams, Polly Toynbee and Simon Jenkins to find Peter Kellner on the screen up in Glasgow elaborating on the final poll YouGov published after the ballot closed (it's now 11.35pm).

No 54%     Yes 46%

Peter says YouGov detected (a) a slight shift to No; and (b) that No voters seemed more determined to turn out. I relax just a tad.

At midnight, sitting in the studio with Andrew and Kate waiting for the programme to switch to us, the Technical Director suddenly roars in. The lights have gone out on the terrace of the Palace of Westminster. 'The BBC has paid good money for those to be kept on,' he curses, with feeling, and rushes out. A few minutes later they come up again. He's made a call.

Say much the same as I did to Jim Naughtie in my first session with Andrew Neill. News has come in that HMQ will release a written statement at 3pm this afternoon. Stress the significance and novelty of this – no precedent. Not like HMQ and general elections in which HMQ has a choreography that is understood – only sending for a party leader when its plain who can command the confidence of the House of Commons.

Dave Gray comes up on the screen from the Pickaquoy Centre in Kirkwall. Looks as if the Orkney count might be the first to declare. In the event it's tiny Clackmannanshire, north of the Firth of Forth, at 1.28am:

35,410 voted; 88.6% turnout
Yes:  16,350   46%
No:  19,036   54%

John Curtice comments in the Glasgow studio that the expectation was that Yes would 'have done somewhat better than this in Clackmannanshire'.

Polly Toynbee and Simon Jenkins are in with Andrew. Polly comes up with a very good line:

We don't have a constitution. You have a lot of barnacles and no boat.

Andrew is on great form but emitting little spurts of fury when whoever is controlling *Scotland Decides* chooses to go to a reporter in a counting centre to repeat what Andrew regards as obvious instead of coming to us in Westminster (Kate Williams and I were sitting with him for nearly an hour before the cameras switched to us).

At 2.03am Orkney declares.

14,907 voted; 83.7 turnout
Yes:  4,883   33%
No:  10,004   67%

Andrew comes into the Green Room and says: 'Well, it's all over. It's becoming an English story now.'

We talk about the YouGov poll on 2 September; how it changed expectations and set new benchmarks, as did the one in *The Sunday Times* on 7 September. Owen Jones, who's waiting to go on, describes it as 'the most influential opinion poll in history'.

There's lightning and heavy rain over the Palace of Westminster. We wonder if this is God showing he's a unionist.

When the Controller finally turns the cameras on Simon Jenkins, he says, cutting against the grain as ever, that if it's a No 'Westminster will shut up shop' rather than go in for recasting the constitution.

Owen Jones says he wants a constitutional convention. Simon says he wants it too. Andrew disagrees with Simon – there is a head of steam building up. Simon says it's a tragedy for England that the union is still in place. Owen: 'There's a need to rebalance the British constitution'. Simon: 'It just isn't going to happen now'.

2.43am. Shetland declares

15,620 voted; 84% turnout
Yes:   5,600   36%
No:    9,951   64%

2.55am. Relief setting in – I hope not prematurely.

Michael Gove says the Conservatives don't want to go down the route of an English Parliament. Jim Murphy [who shortly after the referendum was to become leader of the

Scottish Labour Party] says the decision in Scotland can't go unremarked in England and elsewhere.

3.00am. Western Isles declare.

19,739 voted; 86% turnout
Yes: 9,195  47%
No:  10,544  53%

John Curtice says this is probably the most disappointing result for the Yes campaign so far.

Andy Marr interviews Ming Campbell at the final count centre in Edinburgh. AM says he's heard the Yes campaign are conceding in West Lothian. Ming says it would be 'political suicide' for the two main parties now to do nothing. 'Politics will not be the same again … Some kind of federal solution for the whole UK is inevitable … Scots MPs continuing to vote on English health and education matters now untenable … House of Lords reform would be part of the package'.

I scribble: 'A consensus is building up to carve out an English Parliament inside the Westminster House of Commons.'

Jim Murphy, as impressive as he has been throughout the campaign, says we've got to make a success of whatever has been decided in Scotland.

3.35am. Inverclyde declares.

54,601 voted; 87.4% turnout
Yes: 27,243  49%
No:  27,329  51%

Robert Peston tells Andrew that if it's a clear No vote, sterling will bounce back.

3.54am. Renfrewshire declares.

117,533 voted; 87.2% turnout
Yes: 55,466   47%
No:  62,067   53%

3:55am. Dundee declares.

93,500 voted; 78.8% turnout
Yes: 53,620   57%
No:  39,860   43%

Brian Taylor says it looks like a No outcome. It had to be bigger than that in Dundee. Andy Marr says don't be too definite, even now. Huw Edwards says it's still perfectly possible that it will be a Yes.

The results now pour in. No need to wait until the big one. 4.51am. Glasgow declares.

364,664 voted; 75% turnout
Yes: 194,000  53%
No:  169,347  47%

At 4.56 Nick Robinson says: 'The UK is surviving. There will not be an independent Scotland.' John Curtice agrees with him. It's still 54/46 overall at the moment. Nick wonders if the SNP will join all the other parties in a discussion of the next tranche of devolution.

6.09am. Fife carries No across the line.

I've done my last burst with Andrew (push the need for a convention or a Royal Commission; also suggest that what we have seen about the brittleness of the union could be 'no end of a lesson', as Kipling wrote of the Boer War). He and his team are about the decamp to College Green and I am to go to New Broadcasting House and *Today*.

Big Ben is at 6.16am when the taxi cab carries me past what is now a tent city on College Green on a slightly damp, faintly misty September morning brightened up by pure relief.

*Today* studio with Evan Davis. 7.06am, PM comes out and delivers his Downing Street Declaration. Here's the text:

> The people of Scotland have spoken. It is a clear result. They have kept our country of four nations together. Like millions of other people, I am delighted. As I said during the campaign, it would have broken my heart to see our United Kingdom come to an end.
>
> And I know that sentiment was shared by people, not just across our country, but also around the world because of what we've achieved together in the past and what we can now do together in the future.
>
> So now it is time for our United Kingdom to come together, and to move forward. A vital part of that will be a balanced settlement – fair to people in Scotland and importantly to everyone in England, Wales and Northern Ireland as well.
>
> Let us remember why we had this debate – and why it was right to do so.
>
> The Scottish National Party (SNP) was elected in

Scotland in 2011 and promised a referendum on independence. We could have blocked that; we could have put it off, but just as with other big issues, it was right to take – not duck – the big decision.

I am a passionate believer in our United Kingdom – I wanted more than anything for our United Kingdom to stay together.

But I am also a democrat. And it was right that we respected the SNP's majority in Holyrood and gave the Scottish people their right to have their say.

Let us remember why it was right to ask the definitive question. Yes or No. Because now the debate has been settled for a generation or as Alex Salmond has said, perhaps for a lifetime.

So there can be no disputes, no re-runs – we have heard the settled will of the Scottish people.

Scotland voted for a stronger Scottish Parliament backed by the strength and security of the United Kingdom and I want to congratulate the No campaign for that – for showing people that our nations really are better together.

I also want to pay tribute to Yes Scotland for a well-fought campaign and to say to all those who did vote for independence: 'We hear you'.

We now have a chance – a great opportunity – to change the way the British people are governed, and change it for the better.

Political leaders on all sides of the debate now bear a heavy responsibility to come together and work constructively to advance the interests of people in Scotland, as well as those in England, Wales and Northern Ireland, for each and every citizen of our United Kingdom.

To those in Scotland sceptical of the constitutional promises made, let me say this: we have delivered on devolution under this government, and we will do so again in the next Parliament.

The three pro-union parties have made commitments, clear commitments, on further powers for the Scottish Parliament. We will ensure that they are honoured in full.

And I can announce today that Lord Smith of Kelvin – who so successfully led Glasgow's Commonwealth Games – has agreed to oversee the process to take forward the devolution commitments, with powers over tax, spending and welfare all agreed by November and draft legislation published by January.

Just as the people of Scotland will have more power over their affairs, so it follows that the people of England, Wales and Northern Ireland must have a bigger say over theirs. The rights of these voters need to be respected, preserved and enhanced as well.

It is absolutely right that a new and fair settlement for Scotland should be accompanied by a new and fair settlement that applies to all parts of our United Kingdom. In Wales, there are proposals to give the Welsh government and Assembly more powers. And I want Wales to be at the heart of the debate on how to make our United Kingdom work for all our nations. In Northern Ireland, we must work to ensure that the devolved institutions function effectively.

I have long believed that a crucial part missing from

this national discussion is England. We have heard the voice of Scotland – and now the millions of voices of England must also be heard. The question of English votes for English laws – the so-called West Lothian question – requires a decisive answer.

So just as Scotland will vote separately in the Scottish Parliament on their issues of tax, spending and welfare, so too England, as well as Wales and Northern Ireland, should be able to vote on these issues and all this must take place in tandem with, and at the same pace as, the settlement for Scotland.

I hope that is going to take place on a cross-party basis. I have asked William Hague to draw up these plans. We will set up a Cabinet Committee right away and proposals will also be ready to the same timetable. I hope the Labour Party and other parties will contribute.

It is also important we have wider civic engagement about to improve governance in our United Kingdom, including how to empower our great cities. And we will say more about this in the coming days.

This referendum has been hard fought. It has stirred strong passions. It has electrified politics in Scotland, and caught the imagination of people across the whole of our United Kingdom.

It will be remembered as a powerful demonstration of the strength and vitality of our ancient democracy. Record numbers registered to vote and record numbers cast their vote. We can all be proud of that. It has reminded us how fortunate we are that we are able to settle these vital issues at the ballot box, peacefully and calmly.

Now we must look forward and turn this into the moment when everyone – whichever way they voted – comes together to build that better, brighter future for our entire United Kingdom.

Evan comes to me on the back of the PM's words. I say it's plain that relief is flooding through every one of David Cameron's capillaries. He's laid out a huge constitutional agenda in what future historians will call his 'Downing Street Declaration'. By all means declare what you want to do but don't rush it. So many percussive effects. Needs great care. Push the case for a Constitutional Convention or a Royal Commission.

Home for breakfast and a bath. Back to new BH to wrap up *The Daily Politics* with Andrew Neill again. Say that 24 hours ago we were preoccupied by the dissolution of the kingdom. Now we are faced with a vast constitutional building site for which there is no blueprint and a clock ticking for the new constructions that have been promised. If we Brits have a genius it is for smart muddling through. But this looks like muddling through without the smart.

## The constitutional building site
## & the Kingdom to come

Six weeks on from the referendum, two factors stood out. Scottish politics and, by extension, UK politics were in the process of remaking themselves in a way that was largely, though not wholly, unforeseeable as relief flooded in on Friday 19 September. And, secondly, the three mainstream parties had, so far, singularly failed to rise to the level of events on seeking to remake the British constitution, with the contagion of party advantage infecting both the West Lothian Question and the related English Question.

In the month-and-a-half after the result, the SNP had quadrupled its party membership to over 80,000*, Johann Lamont had resigned as Leader of the Labour Party in Scotland (with accompanying harsh words for Ed Miliband and the London leadership). And a pair of polls in *The Times* over two days (31 October and 1 November) suggested that a huge swathe of Labour seats in Scotland will go to the SNP in May's general election and that if the referendum were re-run it would go the way of independence.

---

* By mid-January 2015, SNP membership was estimated at 92,000 (*The Times*, 16 January 2015). The figures for Labour were 190,000 (across the UK, of course, not just Scotland); Conservative 150,000; Green 44,713; Liberal Democrats 44,526; UKIP 41,943.

A Labour Party *sans* its Scottish bastions would be truly weakened in 2015. A strong majority for the SNP in the Holyrood elections of 2016 would point to another referendum. The electoral geography and the very kingdom itself are in a state of palpable uncertainty.

Here are the polls that reflected this. First YouGov, published in *The Times* on 31 October, on party support in Scotland if there were an imminent general election:

SNP      43%
Labour  27%

Should it happen, that would convert into Labour losing 30 of the 41 Westminster seats it currently holds out of the 59 Scottish MPs. Even worse was an IPSOS MORI poll for STV which put the SNP on 52% and Labour 23%, which would leave Labour with four seats.[13] With its ancient Scottish barbican rubbled, Labour could not hope to form a majority government at Westminster. These polls swelled a sea of rising troubles for Ed Miliband, which the following week led to welling speculation that he might somehow be forced out as Leader, though Labour's internal voting systems are powerfully stacked against this.[14]

It was plain, too, that something quite profound was happening in Scotland, with Labour's woes contrasting with a quadrupling of the membership of the SNP since referendum day. On 1 November, *The Times* published another YouGov poll suggesting that were the referendum re-run it would come out 52% to 48% for independence.[15] Helen Liddell summed it up pithily when the House of Lords debated devolution on 29 October: 'If you read the Scottish press and look at the atmosphere, you would think that No had lost.'[16]

A couple of weeks later a shrewd, historically minded Scottish Labour veteran thought aloud for me about what he called this 'very disruptive period' in Scotland. 'Above the surface,' he said, 'chaos. Then below the surface there is this less discernible social change', which is, he thinks, pushing in the direction of ultimate separation.

He winnowed out a number of factors. The generation who came to their formation in the years after the Second World War, when Britishness was at its height, are diminishing in numbers. The big national industries – coal, steel and shipbuilding – have disappeared or are substantially diminished. And the Thatcher years 'ended the feeling that we're all in this together'.

The referendum, he went on, illustrated a significant change in attitude among the West of Scotland working class, who had been so powerfully affected by the demise of heavy industry. 'Their perceived interest in being British has gone.'

In the past the Irish Catholic element in the Scottish working class 'had the least attachment to the Crown and the Union' but, paradoxically, fear of a Scottish Parliament being a Protestant Parliament had kept them Unionist. But after 15 years' experience of a Scottish Parliament that factor had gone too and removed their fear of separation.[17]

My friend didn't mention the fiscal factor, but there are several in the Labour Party who fear that giving Scotland pretty well all tax-raising powers in the next stage of devolution will shift the ratchet another notch towards eventual independence.

The House of Lords debate on the kingdom to come on 29 October was the first time peers had had a chance to take stock since we all dispersed for the summer in July. The nature of the referendum campaign had plainly scarred several Scottish members. Helen Liddell again:

> Frankly, it was the worst election I have ever seen. It was divisive, it was aggressive, it was thoroughly unpleasant and it did not represent the good people of Scotland, whom we saw weeks beforehand at the Commonwealth Games welcoming the world. And, yes, in some places there was an anti-English feeling ...[18]

There was cross-party and crossbench support in the Lords for a constitutional convention or Royal Commission to look at the wider percussive effects across the UK of the surge of extra powers to Scotland.

Summing up for the Coalition, Jim Wallace left the door open for this, while making it plain that 'there are some things which cannot wait [he was referring to the work of the Smith Commission and the proposed draft legislation before the next election] and to try to [wait] would give rise to allegations of bad faith'.[19]

On the wider canvas, Jim said:

> I make it clear that the Government will consider proposals for the establishment of such a convention because, while debate is needed in both Houses, it is important that we engage with the public as well. We should not simply be continuing our constitution behind closed

doors [i.e. in the Cabinet committee chaired by William Hague] ...[20]

In the aftermath of the debate, the All Party Group on Reform, Decentralisation and Devolution (of which I'm a member) decided to press the three party leaders to meet on a Privy Counsellor basis (the traditional way of them meeting to seek agreement on substantial matters) and press on to get such a convention established.

During the Lords debate, I suggested that this was precisely what they should have done on Friday 19 September, instead of falling out on the question of English votes for English Laws.[21] I also argued that first-order constitutional legislation of the kind proposed for devo-max for Scotland and, if it happens, legislation for further substantial decentralisation in the UK, needs to meet certain tests. It needs to be predictable in its operation and it needs to be durable. 'For that to be achieved, it needs to live and breathe in a stable yet sensitive relationship with the other adjacent moving parts of the constitution.'

Finally, I suggested that, 'There is a prior requirement if these tests are to be met: a high level of parliamentary and, by extension, public consensus. To achieve this takes thought, consultation, care and time.' With the metabolic rate of inter-party competition rising as we approach May's general election, this was going to be difficult to get.[22]

The question of Lords reform has also been added to the great post-referendum building site. David Steel did so deftly during the Lords debate on 29 October. 'I believe', he said:

that we have to move in a more federal direction. That is where a replacement for this House – a senate elected by the component parts of the United Kingdom – makes good sense. It needs all parties, including my own, to rethink their policies on this so that we come up with a proposal for a proper United Kingdom Parliament, where the upper House really represents the component parts of the United Kingdom.[23]

Jim Wallace mentioned this in his summing up as one of the questions needing a response.[24]

Three days later, on 1 November, the embattled Ed Miliband made the Steel proposal his policy when he addressed Labour's North West Conference in Blackpool, wanting Lords reform to be one of the questions discussed at the constitutional convention for which he was calling. His press release suggested, 'Labour wants the new chamber to be based on representation of the regions and the four nations of the United Kingdom to ensure that a much better spread of people from across the country have their voice heard in Westminster'.[25] The BBC website reported Ed Miliband as saying: 'The House of Lords is one of the biggest pieces of unfinished business in our constitution.'[26]

A fundamental remaking of the second chamber had seemed a long way off in the weeks before Christmas 2014, as parliament, counties, regions, cities, localities and the press absorbed first the report of the Smith Commission published on 27 November[27] and then the fruits of William Hague's Cabinet Committee in the shape of the Command Paper, *The Implications of Devolution for England*, on 16 December.[28]

Lord Smith of Kelvin had published inside his deadline and carried 'all five of Scotland's main political parties' (Conservative, Green, Labour, Liberal Democrat and the SNP)[29] with him. Quite a feat of consensus-building. Details in a moment because perhaps what made Lord Smith's report highly unusual were his thoughts on the human geography of what the kingdom is living through. Under the heading of 'Inter-governmental working' he wrote:

> Throughout the course of the Commission, the issue of weak inter-governmental working was repeatedly raised as a problem. That current situation coupled with what will be a stronger Scottish Parliament and a more complex devolution settlement means the problem needs to be fixed. Both Governments need to work together to create a more productive, robust, visible and transparent relationship. There also needs to be greater respect between them. I recommend that the Prime Minister of the UK and the First Minister of Scotland meet shortly after January 25 2015 to agree details of how this will be achieved. I would encourage them to find solutions which will carry the confidence of the public and our civic institutions.[30]

Amen to that. Lord Smith in his 'Foreword' also emphasised that public knowledge of the complexities of the existing devolution arrangements, let alone the settlement to come, is not what it should be.[31]

The five parties signed up to what is formally known as 'The Smith Commission Agreement'. It rests on three pillars:

1. providing a durable but responsive constitutional settlement for the governance of Scotland
2. delivering prosperity, a healthy economy, jobs and social justice
3. strengthening the financial responsibility of the Scottish Parliament[32]

The Heads of Agreement, which include those three pillars, repay careful reading because of the danger of future claims that 'we wuz robbed'. Built into these is the possibility of still more devolution ('... it may be appropriate to devolve further powers beyond those set out in the heads of agreement where doing so would aid the implementation of the consensus reached by the parties in this report') and possible separation ('nothing in this report prevents Scotland becoming an independent country in the future should the people of Scotland so choose').[33]

At the very top of the first pillar of agreement is the statement that: 'UK legislation will state that the Scottish Parliament and Scottish Government are permanent institutions.'[34] That might sound to some ears like entrenched legislation to which the British constitution has, heretofore, been a stranger. It is inconceivable, I think, that any future UK government would pass legislation abolishing the Scottish Parliament and Government. But it is still the constitutional position that no current Westminster Parliament can bind a successor in this or any other matter. So entrenched legislation it cannot be. As Lord Hope of Craighead, former Deputy President of the Supreme Court, who has long experience in the higher posts of the Scottish Judiciary, put it during our BBC Radio 4 conversation for *The Kingdom to Come*: 'The basic constitutional principle is that no Parliament can bind its successors. But I think there's a political dimension to this as well, and the very first words of the Scotland Act 1998 are "There shall be a Scottish Parliament" ... If you want to add the word "permanent" all right, but what do you mean by it? ... It may have some political resonance. But I don't think technically it adds anything.'[35]

Smith pays careful attention to the machinery needed to increase the chances of what I would call the co-operative model, without which the new settlement cannot flourish as it should. He recommends a beefing up of existing joint arrangements, including 'a provision for well-functioning arbitration processes as a last resort', all to be laid out in a 'new and overarching Memorandum of Understanding ... between the UK Government and devolved administrations'. This will be needed not least 'to oversee the implementation and operation of the tax and welfare powers to be devolved by way of this agreement'.[36]

In there, too, are some particular sensitivities touched upon in careful language. For example, hidden away behind pillar 1 under the heading 'Crown Estate' is the clause preventing a future SNP Government from closing the approach waters in the Firth of Clyde to Royal Navy submarines. Under the new settlement, the Scottish economic assets of the Crown Estate will be transferred to the Scottish Parliament but:

The Scottish and UK Governments will draw up and agree a Memorandum of Understanding to ensure that such devolution is not detrimental to UK-wide critical national infrastructure in relation to matters such as defence and security, oil and gas and energy.[37]

Similarly, the licensing of onshore gas and oil extraction will go to the Scottish Parliament but the licensing of offshore oil and gas extraction will remain a UK reserved matter.[38]

Pillar 2 of Smith leaves decisions about state pensions, universal credit and the national minimum wage with the UK Parliament. But the Scottish Parliament will possess new powers to create new benefits and over discretionary payments.[39]

Under the third, 'Financial responsibility', pillar, national insurance contributions inheritance, capital gains and corporation taxes, and the taxation of oil and gas receipts will remain reserved.[40] But problems may well lie ahead with income tax. Under the Smith consensus,

> the Scottish Parliament will have the power to set the rates of Income Tax and the thresholds at which they are paid for ... by Scottish taxpayers

while

> All other aspects of Income Tax will remain reserved to the UK Parliament, including the imposition of the annual charge to income tax, the personal allowance, the taxation of savings and dividend income, the ability to introduce and amend tax reliefs and the definition of income.[41]

That split could prove a serious tension inducer in the future. So could the big questions of borrowing powers and the means of withstanding serious economic shocks. Here the Smith consensus assumes the viability of the co-operative model working through a Joint Exchequer Committee.

Scottish borrowing powers, according to Smith, 'should be agreed by the Scottish and UK Governments, and their operation should be kept under review'.[42] Friction will arise jeopardising what I would call the relative harmony model if the Scottish Government and the UK Government have clear, but different, economic principles. In that case, their assessments of borrowing needs could seriously diverge, threatening to dissolve the fiscal glue that binds the kingdom. Similarly, centrifugal forces are foreseeable in the crisis circumstances the Smith Report captures under the heading 'UK Economic Shocks':

> the UK Government should continue to manage risks and economic shocks that affect the whole of the UK. The fiscal framework should therefore ensure that the UK Government retains the levers to do that, and that the automatic stabilisers continue to work across the UK. The UK Parliament would continue to have a reserved power to levy an additional UK-wide tax if it was felt it was in the UK national interest.[43]

It is the possibility of another major financial crisis and a real-life stress test on the new economic and fiscal arrangements that most worried Alistair Darling when I interviewed him for *The Kingdom to Come* shortly after the Smith

Commission had reported. As Chancellor when the financial storm of 2008 unfolded, he is acutely sensitive to the perils of splitting responsibilities:

> In 2008 I was acutely conscious of that ... Equally ... if you look at welfare, which is going to be a big issue for years to come as the population ages, being part of something bigger means it is much easier then to accommodate and absorb the additional costs. Now once you ... Balkanise that, it becomes much more difficult. Now I don't say it's impossible – far from it – you can do these things. But you do need to make sure in times of stress – because that's always the time that these things get called into question – you need to make sure you know what you're doing.[44]

Alistair Darling, as he made plain in that radio conversation, is a devolver ('I am very enthusiastic about handing powers down') but he's equally aware that 'being part of something bigger means that when you get a shock to the system – whether it's a recession; whether it's a banking crisis – because you are a bigger entity you can better deal with that'.[45]

The more one reads the Smith Report, the more one is struck by just how dependent the Scottish settlement of 2015 will be on the sustenance of a high level of political harmony and institutional co-operation. That extra mutual respect that Lord Smith wishes to see is critical to the viability of the consensus he engineered between the five political parties at his table during the autumn of 2014.

In complete contrast to the Smith consensus was the stark discord between Conservative and Labour on the question of English Votes for English Laws (or EVEL) even before the final result of the Scottish referendum was in. At the turn of 2014–15, EVEL was where the heat and the dust of political clash was most evident.

Alistair Darling was appalled to hear at 5am on the morning of Friday 19 September what the Prime Minister proposed to say outside No.10 about EVEL. When I asked him about it during our conversation, he said:

> I suppose I felt relief about two o'clock in the morning when I could see the results were coming in and it was obvious there was going to be a decisive No vote. However, by five o'clock in the morning when it was clear to me that David Cameron was going to raise the question of English votes for English legislation – then it just seemed to me that the victory that had been won by the majority of people in Scotland was about to be undermined and that Salmond was going to get back in through the front door by [Cameron] announcing this new policy which, to me, had not been thought out, not been developed.[46]

Naturally, William Hague did not see it this way when I interviewed him for the same series of conversations. I asked him if he had any regrets that the English Question 'was politicised in this party way so quickly?' He replied:

> No regrets at all actually. And, of course, people can always blame each other for lack of consensus. Labour politicians can say 'Well, the Conservatives by raising this issue meant that there wasn't a consensus'. We can say, 'It's

Labour's failure to understand that the English Question has to be addressed as well which is preventing a consensus'. So, as ever in politics, you can blame each other for lack of a consensus.

William Hague believes public opinion would have made EVEL an urgent political debate between the referendum and the 2015 general election whatever the position of the political parties:

> What is clear to us is that this issue cannot be avoided. Whether or not the Prime Minister had ... said that we now have to confront the issue of English votes on English laws, it would have been an issue in the general election. People would have made it an issue ... This is a democratic country and people want to raise this issue and they want to know what we're all going to do about it. We have to have that argument.[47]

When Mr Hague presented the Government's Command Paper, *The Implications of Devolution for England*, to the House of Commons in December 2014, it reflected intra-Coalition divisions. Conservative and Liberal Democrat proposals were laid out separately.[48] (The Labour Party had declined to join Mr Hague's Cabinet Committee.) The Liberal Democrats wished to see a high degree of devolution all-round, so in their view, 'attempting to deal with the so-called "West Lothian Question" in isolation for England is likely to raise as many constitutional issues as it settles'. The Lib Dem preference is for a constitutional convention first, as such a convention 'is of crucial importance not only in seeking public consent for major change, but also in ensuring that such change is coherent and properly thought through and does not inadvertently unravel our United Kingdom'.[49]

The Conservatives offered three options on which they would consult and reach a decision before the general election. As outlined in the December 2014 Command Paper, they were as follows:

**Option 1: Reformed consideration of Bills at all stages**

The 2000 Commission on Strengthening Parliament, set up by the Conservative Party and chaired by Lord Norton of Louth, recommended that legislation relating only to England, or to only England and Wales, would only be considered by MPs from those parts of the United Kingdom.

+ A Bill would be certified by the Speaker as applying to a particular part of the UK.
+ Where it related only to England or England or Wales, the Bill would have its second reading in a Grand Committee, comprising all the MPs from the relevant nation(s).
+ The Committee stage would be similarly restricted, and Report and Third Reading would be governed by a convention whereby MPs from other nations did not vote.
+ Bills that dealt exclusively with English matters already devolved to the other nations would proceed entirely through an English-only process.
+ Legislation that covered areas which were both

devolved and reserved would need to pass through two parallel processes, one for each part of the bill.

The key advantage of this proposal is its simplicity and the absence of the need for any new stages in the legislative process.

**Option 2: Reformed Amending Stages of Bills**
The 2008 Democracy Task Force, chaired by the Rt Hon Ken Clarke MP, proposed that the amending stage of legislation relating only to England, or only to England and Wales, would be considered only by MPs from those parts of the United Kingdom.

- It recommended that bills certified as relating solely to English, or English and Welsh matters, would pass as normal at Second Reading.
- The Committee Stage would be taken by those MPs only, in proportion to their party representation in the House of Commons.
- At Report stage the bill would be voted on by those MPs only.
- At Third Reading the Bill would be voted on by the whole House.

The key advantage of this proposal is that it allows MPs from England, or from England and Wales, to have the decisive say over the content of legislation while not excluding MPs from other stages and not introducing any new stages to the legislative process.

## Option 3: Reformed Committee Stage and Legislative Consent Motions

A significantly strengthened version of the McKay Commission proposals could be established. Under this proposal, the Committee stage of legislation relating only to England, or only to England and Wales, would be considered only by MPs from those parts of the United Kingdom. Furthermore those Members would have an effective veto over such legislation.

- Second Reading would be taken as normal by all MPs.
- The Committee stages of English or English and Welsh only bills would be taken in Committee only by MPs from those countries, in proportion to their party representation in the House of Commons.
- This procedure would also apply to the English or English and Welsh parts of bills that contained both English or English and Welsh only clauses, and UK wide clauses.
- Report Stage would be taken as normal by all MPs.
- An English Grand Committee would then vote after Report stage but prior to Third Reading, on a Legislative Consent Motion. English or English and Welsh MPs would therefore be able to grant their consent or veto a bill, or relevant parts of it.
- Such decisions would have the same status as those of the Scottish Parliament on devolved matters. A bill could not pass to Third Reading without passing the legislative consent vote.
- Third Reading would be taken as normal by all MPs,

but only if the legislative consent motion was passed.

• The English Grand Committee could have other functions, including determining the distribution of expenditure within England, such as local government finance or police grants, and it could also have additional questions to Ministers in departments with English-only functions.

• The principle of requiring consent from an English Grand Committee would be applied to levels of taxation and welfare benefits where the equivalent rates have been devolved to Scotland or elsewhere.

The key advantage of this proposal is that it would give English, or English and Welsh MPs, a crucial say over the content of legislation and a secure veto over it passing, while not excluding other MPs from its consideration in the full House of Commons.

Alternative versions of this option include considerations of a Legislative Consent Motion at an earlier stage, before Second Reading, or determining whether or not there is English or English and Welsh consent by means of a double majority system. This would see relevant legislation needing the support of a majority of MPs in the UK but also a majority of MPs from England, or England and Wales.[50]

On 3 February 2015, William Hague announced the Conservative Party's preferred choice to achieve 'English Votes for English Laws' – Option 3, which, he said, 'would include two important innovations in Parliament'. Firstly, at the Committee Stage of a bill that only affected England or England and Wales, the bill would only be considered by MPs from England or England and Wales 'chosen in proportion to party strength in England, or England and Wales when appropriate'. The second innovation 'would add a new stage to how legislation is passed. That would comprise a Grand Committee made up of all English MPs, or all English and Welsh MPs.'

Mr Hague explained that:

No Bill or part of a Bill relating only to England would be able to pass its third reading and become law without being approved in such a Grand Committee. This involves asking the English or English and Welsh MPs for their consent through a legislative consent motion. If they refused to pass it, then it could ... be referred back to the House of Commons for further negotiation. But no such Bill could be passed without their consent. At all other stages of legislation all other MPs would remain involved.[51]

The Conservatives' proposal stimulated an impassioned philippic the following day from Gordon Brown, in what many thought might be his last great speech in the House before stepping down as an MP ahead of the 2015 general election. He tore into the Conservatives' EVEL approach: 'In retaliation for what they see as Scots pursuing a Scottish interest, they wish to pursue and enshrine an English interest above a common UK interest that could bind us together.'[52] He finished by returning to David Cameron's Downing Street declaration on the morning of Friday 19 September 2014:

On 19 September 2014, for purely short-term gain – putting party before country, without considering the long-term interests of our united country, and ignoring the need to reconcile people and bring them together – he may have lit a fuse that eventually blows the Union apart.[53]

Over the weekend that followed, Nicola Sturgeon denounced the Hague EVEL proposals as 'an affront to the very idea of the UK as a partnership of equals because it cannot be right to exclude Scottish MPs from decisions that have a clear effect on Scotland'.[54]

With the general election visible on the horizon, the nation seemed far, far away from what the former Attorney General, Dominic Grieve, called building 'amity structures within the Union'.[55]

What about the wider question of building a new constitutional roof over the UK as a whole?[56] What chance of a wider look at the whole of the constitution?

As the year turned, the Labour and Liberal Democrat parties were pledged to a Constitutional Convention. The Conservatives were too, but as a drawer-together of all the threads. As expressed in the Command Paper:

### Constitutional Convention

The Conservative Party believes that any future constitutional convention or commission should be concerned with the effective working of the constitutional arrangements for each part of the Union, including the new arrangements for England, to build a better and fairer settlement within our United Kingdom.

Such a body could consider the case for a 'Statute of the Union' to enshrine and reinforce the constitutional arrangements for each part of the Union, and to assist in achieving a stable, long-term settlement across the United Kingdom.

The establishment of any such convention or commission should not delay the implementation of the Smith Commission in Scotland and equivalent changes in the rest of the United Kingdom, including the introduction of English Votes for English Laws, or English and Welsh Votes for English and Welsh Laws.[57]

When I asked him about the case for a constitutional convention in our conversation, William Hague gave a 'not yet' reply:

The danger in the idea of a constitutional commission is that it is produced at the moment as a reason for delay and by people who can't think on earth what to do ... So I have a natural suspicion of that. I would simply say that any constitutional convention has to take place after certain changes we've now set in train. The commitment to Scotland is very clear and must be honoured – and it will be very important to make sure that the necessary consequences for the rest of the UK that flow from that are honoured, are responded to, on the same timetable ... So I don't want to see a constitutional convention that holds all that up. Any conversation would therefore have to be something that built on those changes. Since that's unlikely to be the end of change ... then I think saying a constitutional convention that works from where we've arrived at in a couple of years – well, you can make a case for that.[58]

Plainly, May 2015 is going to be a constitutional general election to a significant degree (which is highly unusual for the UK) – with a swirl of the English Votes for English Laws question and, looming loftily and unpredictably above all, the question of whether or not there will be a referendum on the UK's membership of the European Union during the course of the next Parliament.

In the meantime, Scottish politics has been remaking itself. Membership of the SNP had at least quadrupled between Referendum Day and Hogmanay. Scottish Labour had acquired a new Leader in Jim Murphy on 13 December – his task to halt and then reverse the decline of the Labour Party in Scotland. The referendum and its aftermath struck Scottish Labour a hammer blow that had cruelly exposed weaknesses and fractures long in the making. ICM's online poll of 1,004 Scottish adults was published the day after Boxing Day under *The Guardian's* headline of 'Labour faces Scotland bloodbath'.[59] John Curtice, who helped with the analysis, told the paper 'we are prospectively looking at the collapse of citadels that have always been Labour since the 1920s. That will seem incredible to some in England, but to those of us who paid close attention to Alex Salmond's 2011 landslide [in elections to the Scottish Parliament] at Holyrood, it would merely be the next chapter in the political transformation of a nation. It is becoming clear that the independence referendum has reset all the dials.'

As *The Guardian's* Tom Clark and Severin Carrell reported the ICM findings:

> The Scottish National Party, which took only 20% of the vote in the 2010 general election, has subsequently more than doubled its vote to reach a commanding 43% of the prospective poll next May.
>
> Scottish Labour, which secured a very strong 42% in Gordon Brown's homeland last time around, has since tumbled by 16 points to just 26%.
>
> The Conservatives sink from 2010's 17% to 13%, while the great bulk of the 19% share that the Liberal Democrats scored last time around is wiped out as they fall by 13 points to 6%.
>
> On a uniform swing, these results ... would entirely redraw the political map. Labour's band of 41 Scottish MPs would be reduced to a parliamentary rump of just 10 members ...

But, according to John Curtice, assuming a uniform swing in Scotland may be misleading. As *The Guardian* writers report him:

> By breaking ICM's data into four different categories of seat, Curtice reveals Labour's decline is sharpest in those supposedly heartland seats where it previously trounced the SNP by more than 25 points.
>
> Whereas Labour's Scotland-wide vote drops by 16 points, it falls by 22 points in these constituencies, while the SNP surges by 26. That combination is sufficient

to wipe out majorities that were always assumed to be impregnable, and Scottish Labour's Westminster caucus is left shrivelling to just three MPs.[60]

The Lib Dems, on the assumption of a universal swing, will be down to Alistair Carmichael in Orkney and Shetland, Charles Kennedy in Ross, Skye and Lochaber and Michael Moore in Berwickshire, Roxburgh and Selkirk.[61]

On this projection, one of the Lib Dem seats that will fall to the SNP will be Gordon in Aberdeenshire. If that happens it will propel Alex Salmond back into the House of Commons as an MP. In an interview with *The Independent* on 19 December 2014 he said he 'would lay odds on a balanced Parliament. That's an opportunity to have delivered to Scotland what we have been promised', and give the SNP at Westminster a chance of championing what he called 'progressive values' such as the living wage and opposing the Trident successor programme. He said he drew his inspiration from Charles Stewart Parnell in the 1880s using his parliamentary muscle to further the cause of Irish Home Rule.[62] The SNP would not come to the aid of David Cameron and the Conservatives in the circumstances of a hung parliament at Westminster. Why? 'We won't give succour, help, assistance to the Conservative Party and the reason is David Cameron waltzing out of Downing Street and showing his true face the morning after the referendum.'[63]

The friability and volatility of UK politics as the Scottish, English and UK-wide questions mix and fail to match was evident in the week when the Coalition published the draft clauses of the post-Smith Commission Scotland Bill on

22 January 2015. David Cameron travelled to Edinburgh to launch the command paper, *Scotland in the United Kingdom: An enduring settlement*[64] and to meet Nicola Sturgeon, Scotland's new First Minister. Nicola Sturgeon instantly demonstrated why there should have been a question mark after the words 'An enduring settlement'. She declared that the draft clauses represented a 'significant watering down' of the agreed Smith proposals and that the legislation did not 'represent the meaningful progress on the devolution of the powers we need to design a social security system that meets Scotland's needs'. What irked her in particular was the requirement that Holyrood seek the permission of the Secretary of State for Scotland if it wished to alter housing benefit. David Cameron came back with the accusation that the SNP were trying to undermine the Smith-brokered deal as part of their efforts to 'break up the United Kingdom'.[65]

The day before the publication of the command paper, Nicola Sturgeon had made it plain that the SNP planned to abandon its self-denying ordinance on not voting on English legislation in the Westminster Parliament. This stoked speculation that the SNP were positioning themselves to do a deal over some kind of support for a minority Labour government in London after the May 2015 election and fears that this would stoke English nationalism still further.[66] One Labour veteran said that such a desire on the part of the SNP would be a powerful drummer-up of votes for the Conservatives in English constituencies.[67]

A constitutional steady state seemed – and was – increasingly far off. In an attempt to bring a measure of thoughtfulness and careful process to the melée, the All Party Group on Reform, Decentralisation and Devolution in the United Kingdom unveiled in January 2015 a draft of a proposed manifesto text for all the main UK parties. It reads as follows:

> We will establish a UK Constitutional Convention to mark the 800th anniversary of Magna Carta in 2015. The Convention will operate independent of government and will include members of the public as well as representatives of the political parties, local authorities and the nations and regions of the UK. Members of the public will make up more than half of the total membership.
>
> Sitting for no longer than a year, the Convention will consider and publish recommendations on:
>
> - the relationship between the nations and all parts within the UK, including their fair representation in the Westminster Parliament.
> - arrangements for the governance of England; and
> - other issues that may require the attention of a successor Convention.
>
> We will bring before Parliament proposals to respond to the recommendations of the Convention within six months of its reporting.

William Hague kindly attended the All Party Group meeting. Again, he was distinctly tepid about the idea of a constitutional convention saying: 'A case can be made for a constitutional convention. It's not something we reject out of hand.'

I asked him if he could perhaps show a touch more enthusiasm for the idea and he laughed and said: 'I thought I was actually being forward leaning.'

He explained that he did not want such a convention to be an excuse to delay English votes for English laws.

None of us think our constitutional development will have come to an end in 2016. I am suspicious of a constitutional convention that stops everything in England.

By contrast, Michael Forsyth (Lord Forsyth of Drumlean), Secretary of State for Scotland in John Major's Cabinet, said of the draft Scotland Bill that, 'I regard it less as a milestone; it is probably more likely to be a tombstone for the United Kingdom if we continue in this way by making piecemeal constitutional reform'.[68] And the focus on electoral possibilities and the general racing of pulses that always accompanies election campaigns added to the feeling of the UK's living in a whirlpool of multiple, overlapping uncertainties.

All this adds up to a Rubik's Cube of possibilities beyond the May 2015 general election. We could even move from our familiar 2¼ party system (with the Liberal Democrats as the quarter) to a genuine multi-party system, almost as if we had become a proportional-representation nation, particularly as UKIP could well siphon off traditional Labour votes in some of the old industrial heartlands as well as a scattering of the neglected coastlands. What a time to be remaking the internal constitutional arrangements of the kingdom to come.

So what questions must we face as a people and a polity if we are to have a chance of finishing up with a settlement that produces a kingdom whose constituent parts can live in a condition of mutual flourishing?

# Mutual flourishing?

Scotland remains *the* constitutional question. As Lord Smith of Kelvin made plain in his report, the consensus he crafted from the five-party discussions could be just a way-station to either what one might call devo-max-max, or to complete independence. The 'Neverendum' syndrome, as the Canadians came to call their sequence of referenda on the Quebec question, could develop here. Just think of the fuse the following outcomes would light once more under the United Kingdom:

- 30–40 SNP members elected to the Westminster Parliament in May 2015
- SNP win another outright majority in the Scottish Parliament in the Holyrood elections of May 2016, with another referendum as the party's top election pledge
- At some point between 2016 and 2020 the UK as a whole votes in a referendum to leave the European Union while the vote in Scotland is strongly to stay in

In my judgement, that would mean a second independence referendum in the 2020s, which could well go the way of separation.

In other words, not only is Scotland likely to remain in a condition of political inflammation (even without the European ingredient), the survival of the UK in its present form remains a live question.

Let us for a moment assume that the new, Smith-shaped settlement for Scotland is in place with all the necessary legislative underpinning in the spring or summer of 2016. There exists the possibility that economic disturbance of a serious kind (Eurozone or global-recession induced or something less foreseeable) will pummel the UK by 2020 if not sooner. Such an occurrence could well apply the economic and fiscal stress test to the new Anglo-Scottish financial membranes that Alistair Darling has spoken of. The global economy can be a thing of swiftness and brutality; it would be both blind and deaf to the needs and sensitivities of a United Kingdom still striving to make its new internal deal work.

By then new deals could well be under negotiation on further devolution to Wales and Northern Ireland and on decentralisation within England. And the very institution in which the high policy will play out and in which the needed legislation shaped – Parliament – could well be in a state of reconstruction. Will we see the formation of a surrogate English Parliament within the existing House of Commons? Will blueprints be in production for a House of Lords completely remade as a Senate for the Nations and Regions, with its members either directly elected or indirectly elected by the parliaments, assemblies, regions, city statelets, clusters of counties and towns – or whatever patchwork quilt emerges to clothe the English landscape? And will we achieve what the philosopher Onora O'Neill, Baroness O'Neill of

Bengarve, called 'Devo-coherence' with such a likely variety of authorities?[69]

Other institutions may be morphing as a result of this picture of multiple, rolling change. Can a unified civil service be sustained under devo-max for Scotland, with easy interchanges of official talent between all parts of the kingdom? Robin Butler, Lord Butler of Brockwell, the former Cabinet Secretary and Head of the Home Civil Service, described the unified civil service as 'one of the bits of glue that holds the kingdom together just like the Armed Forces and other services of the Crown' adding that he couldn't see why the tradition of serving different administrations shouldn't continue under devo-max. 'We're used to conflicting loyalties', he said when I talked to him for *The Kingdom to Come*.[70]

Another institutional worry could be that the Supreme Court, which arbitrates in disputes about powers between the devolved administrations and Westminster/Whitehall, might become politicised if devolution-related business rose as a proportion of its workload. Lord Hope of Craighead, its former Deputy President, thinks that can be avoided:

> The Court looks at the language of the statute under which the issue arises. And it [will be] interpreting the statute and applying it in the way that the Court has always done – and that's not a political exercise, it's a judicial exercise. And the individuals who are sitting there are chosen entirely independently of government now and there's no question of them having a political angle on this at all. So I would hope that people wouldn't try to politicise it.[71]

So do I.

Is there lurking here a great opportunity to break the habits of a national lifetime and go for a written constitution to pull the threads together? Graham Allen MP, the Labour chairman of the House of Commons Political and Constitutional Reform Committee, has led his colleagues through the possible ways of doing so if Parliament and people so wished.[72] And the President of the Supreme Court, Lord Neuberger, touched on the possibility in October 2014. 'I think', he told a gathering of lawyers in Bangor, 'it is not inappropriate to raise the question, and I emphasise that it is genuinely no more than raising the question, of whether the time has come for the United Kingdom to have a constitution'.[73]

Lord Neuberger rehearsed the pros and cons including the argument that:

> we have managed very well for many centuries without a constitution, so why mend it if it ain't broken? It is beguiling to invoke the existence of successful constitutions of other countries, but it is plain that what works very well in one country may not take root successfully in another. The British constitutional system has developed on a piecemeal basis, and to impose a written constitution on such a system is, some may think, a questionable exercise: it could be said to risk forcing an inherently flexible system into an artificial straightjacket.

'But', he continued, 'there are powerful arguments the other way.'

First, we are in a new world whose increasing complexity appears to require virtually every activity and organisation to have formal rules as to how it is to be run and to work, and there is no obvious reason why that should not apply to the most important organisation of the lot. Secondly, we are now in what to some people might seem to be in an unsatisfactory position with an international treaty, as interpreted by an international court, namely the European Convention on Human Rights, acting as a semi-constitution.[74]

(It's worth noting in passing that at the 2014 Conservative Conference, David Cameron pledged to establish a new British Bill of Rights.)[75]

Lord Neuberger summed up in a long but beautifully balanced paragraph:

We have a proud and successful history with a pragmatic, rather than principled, approach to law and legal systems, and we have managed pretty well without a constitution. But times change, and the fact that we managed well without a constitution in a very different world from that which we now inhabit may be a point of limited force when applied to the present. So long as things remained much the same, the argument based on the status quo was hard to resist. However, if, and it's a big 'if' which is ultimately a political decision, our system of government is going to be significantly reconsidered and restructured, there is obviously a more powerful case for a written constitution. Writing a constitution may help focus minds on the details of the restructuring, and, once the reconstructing has occurred, a new formal constitution should provide the new order with a clarity and certainty which may otherwise be lacking. On the other hand, it remains the case that grafting a written constitution onto our pragmatic system would almost inevitably involve something of a leap in the dark, and many people may fear that it would turn out to be a classical example of a well-intentioned innovation which had all sorts of unintended and undesired consequences.[76]

In my view, it's highly unlikely that an overarching written British constitution will coagulate out of the kingdom to come however first-order and fundamental some of the questions we face. The Scottish settlement will have its statute. There is a strong possibility that House of Commons procedure will be adapted to facilitate some version of EVEL. There is, too, a definite likelihood of a convention after those developments are properly underway to, as it were, mop up the rest and fashion an overarching constitutional settlement that captures the multiple changes as coherently as possible.

For me such a constitutional convention must approach its task with a particular state of mind about the need to enable both mutual flourishing and a capacity for the UK to think and act together as a Union, as a collectivity amongst all the devolution and decentralisation. It's crucial for the shared future of those who live in these islands that we should not Balkanise ourselves, in either structural terms or in our minds and hearts – for that way lies friction, fragmentation and discord.

Never before in recent times have constitutional possibility and peril jostled together quite like this. Despite the 55/45 result in the Scottish referendum, there is more uncertainty lying upon the kingdom to come than at any peacetime moment in the memories of the Queen's subjects. The British constitution, with its mix of statutes, codes, custom, precedent and tacit understandings,[77] may still baffle but it has ceased to bore. Refashioning it successfully and enduringly is going to take immense care and thought, plus a high level of consensus within the political parties and between the constituent parts of the kingdom. With time, intelligence and forbearance all round, it can be done in a way that serves the needs of the generations to come. If it is botched, they will curse us – and rightly so – for they will have to live with the consequences.

# Part two

# Referendum diary

## Friday 8 August: Last thoughts from South Ronaldsay

What still shocks me as I look south from the Orkneys is the failure of the Scottish Question to take fire in England generally and Whitehall in particular. This was apparent even (with a few exceptions) within the private inner recesses of government. Last month, the Cabinet Secretary, Sir Jeremy Heywood, confirmed that departments in the UK Civil Service were undertaking no contingency planning for the consequences of a Scottish vote to separate, holding firm to a Cabinet decision at the turn of 2012–13 that there should be none (not that Sir Jeremy referred in public to the Cabinet decision; Cabinet Secretaries don't do that sort of thing). In a July interview with Matt Ross for *Civil Service World*, Heywood explained that:

> Ministers have said no contingency planning. Effectively, the government is very confident it's going to win the argument on this, but in the end it's a matter for the people of Scotland to decide.

Asked about the consequences of a Yes, Sir Jeremy said '… I think we'll have whatever time is needed to respond to the outcome'.[78]

An SNP government in an independent Edinburgh

deciding to uphold its pledge to remove all UK nuclear weapons and their submarine carriers from Scottish waters could effectively finish the remainder of the UK (RUK, as Whitehall calls it), as a nuclear weapons state unless an extra £20 billion and a construction programme of 20 years was set in train, with the US Government agreeing to host our submarines in its King's Bay, Georgia base in the interim. But no civil servant in the Ministry of Defence could commit those thoughts to even the most highly classified pieces of paper the department circulates internally. In some Whitehall circles the prohibition on contingency planning was referred to as 'the Papal Bull'.[79]

The argument in defence of this decision, as it was whispered to me in early 2013, went like this:

> If we make contingency plans for Scottish independence, their existence will leak. Then Alex Salmond will say 'Look, it's viable. They are preparing for it'.[80]

Two things struck me when I heard this explanation. First, Coalition ministers were allowing themselves to be mesmerised by Scotland's First Minister. And second, that the decision amounted to a dereliction of duty. One of the prime purposes of government is to plan for the possible and to scan the horizon for the unlikely. But for the very configuration of the kingdom as we have known it since 1707? Keep out please. Don't touch it. Extraordinary.

How might Friday 19th September transpire if Scotland votes Yes? The Prime Minister will fly to Scotland to see the Queen. Might other senior ministers go too in case a meeting of the Privy Council is thought fitting? The Prince of Wales will no doubt receive swift and full briefings.

A later cataract of information and briefing will go out to Commonwealth Governors-General, UK High Commissioners and Ambassadors abroad for onward transmission to heads of government.

All three party conferences may be cancelled (Labour's is due to start on Saturday 20th September).

From the moment it becomes plain that the vote is going to be yes, the Treasury and the Bank of England will actively try to reassure the financial markets and international financial institutions (with, one wonders, what degree of success?). Given the existing, pre-18 September volatility, the Treasury and the Bank could very well be faced with a run on the pound and a flight of capital. This will have been fuelled by Scottish-based companies, banks and financial institutions announcing their intention to leave.

On the defence side, a statement will no doubt be put out, assuring allies that the Trident patrol cycle and continuous at-sea deterrence will not be disrupted. Early discussions with Nato countries will have been promised, ditto the European Union, with special thought given to the handling of those countries most opposed to Scottish Independence (like Spain for its Catalonian reasons).

The clock will tick furiously on the overseas and currency fronts and set a fast pace for the choreography of the first few days of a kingdom set to sunder. Preparing for the creation of a new and independent state apparatus in Scotland and a rejigged Remainder of UK will require movement across several fronts between 19 September and Christmas 2014:

- Creation of shadow independent Scottish Government departments in areas formerly reserved to Westminster and Whitehall – finance, foreign affairs (including the naming of Scottish shadow ambassadors/high commissioners for the new Scottish Foreign Service), defence, welfare, energy. (This, of course, would be for Edinburgh to do, not London.)

- The creation of a Scottish Civil Service and the abandonment of the UK-wide unified public service and a termination of the Scotland Office.

- Preparation for the removal of a substantial number of UK Civil Service jobs in Scotland especially defence, Department for International Development and HM Revenue and Customs.

- Decisions about who will people and lead the Remainder of the UK team to negotiate with 'Team Scotland' and fix dates for the likely succession of Cameron-Salmond bilateral meetings that would be necessary. Decide if, when and how to persuade the SNP Government that their 18-month timetable for reaching independence is unrealistic.

- Prepare for the handling of independent Scotland's wish to join the EU and Nato before it achieves sovereignty (only governments that are in existence – not just in prospect – can negotiate such successions).

- The setting in train of planning for the longer-term removal of the Royal Navy Submarine Service and attendant facilities from Faslane/ Coulport to somewhere in the Remainder of the United Kingdom.

♦ Get ready for a withdrawal of UK secret service cover for Scotland.

On top of all these moving parts rests a swathe of difficult constitutional questions. Status and role of HM Queen in a post-independence Scotland? Would Scotland become her sixteenth Realm? Would there need to be a Governor-General in Edinburgh?

A Scotland on the road to independence will still return 59 MPs to Westminster after the May 2015 general election. Will they – should they? – be allowed to speak and vote on the terms and clauses of what might be called the Scotland (Independence) Act 2016, 2017 or 2018? Scottish members of the House of Lords will also face departure unless they are – or decide to become – domiciled for tax purposes in the Remainder of the UK.

What on earth would the RUK call itself?

### Tuesday 12 August 2014

A YouGov poll in yesterday's *Sun*[81] suggests that the Yes campaign lost out amid the mêlée of possibilities swirling about the shiningly successful Commonwealth Games in Glasgow and the first of the Alex Salmond v Alistair Darling debates that took place a couple of days after the closing ceremony. With the 'Don't Knows' removed, YouGov suggests it's 61 per cent No, 39 per cent Yes – roughly where it came out in its last poll in June.

In the minutes before Salmond v Darling, Round 1 on 4 August, an IPSOS MORI poll showed a 58/42 split. To my, and I suspect, other people's surprise, Alistair Darling came out on top largely because he skewered Salmond on the currency question. Darling managed to appear cross and authoritative at the same time. Looking back at the notes I scribbled as they slugged it out I find not long *before* the currency moment:

Salmond doesn't seem as jaunty as usual. Alistair more animated than usual.

AS evasive on Plan B [for the currency]. AD truly animated now (and continues to be so).

AS pathetic on driving on the right; attacks from outer space [scare stories he claims have been put out by the 'No' campaign].

Truly unedifying from AS.

By my reckoning, the First Minister's performance deteriorated still further when the audience put its questions.

There is a streak of combined smugness and nastiness in AS. (Some of the audience pick up on his snideness and playing the individual when he can't answer the question.)

Pleased and relieved that Alistair did so well.

There was virtual unanimity in the media that Darling really had done well and that the great debater – the dominating figure in the Scottish Parliament who uses Holyrood and First Minister's Questions to such great and sustained effect – had definitely come off second best to Darling, a still rather than sparkling bottle on the shelf of Scottish politicians (though Salmond certainly didn't sparkle on the night).

### Wednesday 13 August 2014

Tam Dalyell rings first thing to talk about last night's BBC2 programme *Scotland votes – What's at stake for the UK?* (for which I recorded an interview in May). Tam says: 'It's getting very fraught up here. I don't know which ways it's going to go.'

The programme, presented by Andrew Neil and produced by Adam Grimley, was especially good on the intricacies of separation (on which Gus O'Donnell [former Cabinet Secretary] and Robert Hazell [Head of the Constitution Unit at UCL] were very fluent) as well as on the big questions like the consequences of an independent Scottish government insisting on the closure of Faslane/Coulport, the Royal Navy's Clyde submarine base. David Trimble was forceful on his fear that Scottish independence, if it came, could turn the dormant question of a united Ireland into a live one once more.

Talk to a well-placed Conservative friend who tells me his party strategists fear that in the aftermath of a No vote, a goodly number of Scottish voters, in a fit of conscience, might return a swathe of SNP MPs to Westminster in next May's general election. This would complicate the picture for the Conservatives if they finished up once more as the largest single party in a hung parliament. Interesting speculation.

Later bump into an old Scottish Labour friend in a near-deserted (bar tourists) House of Lords. I remark on how well Alistair Darling had done in last week's debate. 'You could waterboard Alistair and he would not divert from the line', he replied. 'Alistair's been focussing on the currency question for ages. His private polling must have been telling him that this is what's been worrying people.'

I mentioned to my friend that I thought Alex Salmond had been off form pretty well from the beginning of the debate.

Salmond's reputation had protected him so far as the most impressive and best politician in Scotland by a long way, which is the way that the Scottish media had always presented him. He was also not used to appearing before audiences that he couldn't manipulate – and he couldn't control that audience. The Scottish media had conspired in all this then [after the debate] they turned on him very quickly.

Bit like Harold Wilson in 1963–66. Couldn't put a foot wrong after becoming Leader of the Opposition until the July measures of 1966 took the shine instantly off his economic policies – the very turf of his greatest professional prowess, just as debating flair was until last week seen as *the* Salmond gift.

I banged on a bit last night on the television programme about the bruising and souring effects of all this on what one might call the Anglo-Scottish question. Even if it is a No on 18 September – a convincing No at that – it will have scored a line across the history of the UK. It will not be the same on the other side of the line.

This is why the Ming Campbell idea of a pretty well instant 'Conference of a New Scotland'[82] is so important, as are Bob Maclennan's and the new All-Party Group's* call for a UK-wide constitutional convention.

Last week I had a chat with the MSP for Orkney, Liam Mac-Arthur, about this on Burray and a brief word with the Secretary of State for Scotland, Alistair Carmichael, who has taken up Ming's idea, on the bus that took us from our plane to the terminal in Edinburgh. We'll need a wide and rolling national conversation about all that this autumn to get us beyond the bruises, the recriminations and clear of that cataract of complaint directed at Westminster and Whitehall which over the decades has come increasingly commonplace from certain parts of Scottish politics. Games will need to be raised all round.

### Friday 15 August 2014

Wonderful swipe from Simon Jenkins in this morning's *Guardian* at those of us who had talked about the nuclear deterrent, Faslane and Scottish independence in Andrew Neil's Tuesday-evening programme. Our language, wrote Simon, 'was that of faded imperialists out of their time.'[83] Delicious. Brought me a dash of consolation for having been too young to work as a District Commissioner!

---

* The All-Party Group on Further Decentralisation and Devolution in the United Kingdom was launched by its co-chairs Lord Foulkes of Cumnock and Lord Purvis of Tweed in Church House, Westminster on 11 June 2014.

A TNS poll published on Wednesday, whose field-work was carried out during the Commonwealth Games in Glasgow, with some interviews after the August 5th televised debate, measured the No vote at 45 per cent (up four points over a month) and 32 per cent Yes (no change) with 23 per cent undecided (down two points).[84]

John Redwood received a fair amount of coverage for sallying forth on the English question on Tuesday evening, making the case for intra-English devolution and linking it with his Euroscepticism.

> Should, against all the odds, Scotland vote for independence then the rest of the UK will need a new constitutional settlement, which will emerge from the negotiations over separation. It would also accelerate the need for the renegotiation of our EU relationship. One of the reasons why many English people are Eurosceptic is they have a feeling the EU wants to remove their country from the map of Europe through strokes of the legislative pen and through administrative decisions which ignore, counter-order or bypass our country.[85]

John said that if Scotland votes No we might need a new First Minister of England and an English Parliament that would sit in the House of Commons with Scottish MPs prevented from voting on devolved matters and prohibited from serving as Health or Education Secretaries.[86]

We're going to hear much more 'England Arise' whatever happens.

## Sunday 17 August 2014

Talk to Tam Dalyell on the phone, following up our brief chat on Wednesday. He and Kathleen, Tam said, think 'there's a helluva reason for anxiety. I think there's a considerable danger that it's not going to be all right. All these youngsters who have been canvassed have no conception of the havoc it would cause. Divorce, if it happens, is going to go very sour. I think there would be a run on sterling straight away and the English will be furious.'

Tam has been anxious for decades. He recalled the late 1960s when the Conservatives, then in opposition, moved towards the idea of a Scottish Assembly and he talked to Iain Macleod, Reggie Maudling and Enoch Powell about it.

'Tam, none of my doing', said Macleod.

'Trouble, old boy. Trouble', said Maudling.

'Folly', said Enoch.*

The great Tom Devine has come out in favour of a Yes in this morning's *Observer* as 'there's very little left in the Union except sentiment, history and family'. Tom says he finally made up his mind only over the past fortnight. Previously he'd been a devo-max man but,

---

* Tam told me about he and Enoch coinciding in the Commons Table Office in pursuit of parliamentary questions. Tam's was on the Falklands and he said to Enoch he and the clerks needed a knowledge of iambics to get it right. 'You need a knowledge of iambics for everything in life', said Enoch, and walked straight out erect, as if nothing more needed to be said.

The Scottish parliament has demonstrated competent government and it represents a Scottish people who are wedded to a social-democratic agenda and the kind of political values which sustained and were embedded in the welfare state of the late 1940s and 1950s.

It is the Scots who have succeeded most in preserving the British idea of fairness and compassion in terms of state support and intervention. Ironically, it is England, since the 1980s, which has embarked on a separate journey.

There's also the weakening influence of the monarch and the absence of an external and potentially hostile force which once would have induced internal collective solidarity, such as fascism and the Soviet empire.[87]

The Australian Prime Minister, Tony Abbott, could have put it better yesterday when, in a *Times* interview with Tim Montgomerie, he began well. The Scottish Enlightenment, he said, was the 'intellectual foundation for so much of what's best in the modern world ... What the Scots do is a matter for the Scots and not for a moment do I presume to tell Scottish voters which way they should vote.'

Then came the unfortunate bit in the second sentence of what followed:

But as a friend of Britain, as an observer from afar, it's hard to see how the world would be helped by an independent Scotland. I think that the people who would like to see the break-up of the United Kingdom are not the countries whose company one would like to keep.[88]

The papers report that Alex Salmond will be in Arbroath today to deliver his own version of The Declaration of 1320, which denounced English attempts to subjugate Scotland:

> for as long as but a hundred of us remain alive, we shall never on any conditions be subjected to English rule. It is in truth not for glory, nor riches, nor honours that we fight, but for freedom alone, which no honest man gives up except with his life.[89]

This weekend's *Economist* takes a thoughtful, longer look at the Scottish Question – the possibility that post a No result, Scotland will fall into a state of '"neverendum"; the term applied to Quebec's decades-long deliberations about breaking from Canada. Better Together will disband after 18 September whereas the Yes campaign is a movement ... [which] ... has flushed blood into the muscles of Scottish nationalism'.[90]

A month to go – and still England hasn't awoken to the magnitudes bound up inside a Yes vote. Wilson's Law is having its customary deadening effect. This is the tag I've applied to the former Cabinet Secretary Richard Wilson's idea that the British go into their big constitutional changes 'as if under anaesthetic'. Only later do they wake up and say, 'Did we really mean it to be like that?' Richard had in mind in particular the UK's accession to the European Economic Community in 1973. I reckon the anaesthetic is swirling around in considerable quantities south of the Cheviots. Will it disperse to any significant degree over the next few weeks?

## Monday 18 August 2014

A *Times* YouGov poll this morning reveals what Peter Kellner, YouGov's chairman, calls 'a real shift of opinion, especially among Scots under 40' in favour of a Yes vote. The figures are:

51%  No
38%  Yes
11%  Undecided

which, stripped of the undecideds and the non-voters produces 57/43, 'four points up on the week'.[91] This strikes me more as a reversion to the pre-debate position than a turning-point, though I must confess to a tinge of anxiety.

*The Times* also runs a story on its front page speculating than an independent Scotland might run a referendum on the headship of state once the Queen has died. The piece also speculates on possible embarrassment for HMQ with different advice being given to her on a question where Edinburgh and London are in serious disagreement.

Robert Blackburn, Professor of Constitutional Law at King's, suggests a Governor-Generalship for Scotland might be the way round that.[92] Vernon Bogdanor, cited in the same article, reckons (as I do) that the Queen's views haven't changed since she addressed both Houses of Parliament in her Jubilee Year 1977 and touched on the question, as it was then, of possible devolution to Scotland and Wales:

> I number kings and queens of England and of Scotland and princes of Wales among my ancestors and so I can readily understand these aspirations. But I cannot forget

that I was crowned Queen of the United Kingdom of Great Britain and Northern Ireland.

I remember the very real impact of that last sentence at the time. The Scottish nationalists were not pleased and HMQ's words were widely seen as significant. As far as I know, she's not said anything comparable since. As somebody well placed in Whitehall said to me a couple of months ago of the Queen, 'She'll be doing her bit on 4 July', the day she named the new aircraft carrier *HMS Queen Elizabeth* in a stirring ceremony in a chilly wind at rainswept Rosyth (which certainly warmed up the cockles of this old faded imperialist's heart watching it a few feet away from HMQ in the stand).

### Tuesday 19 August 2014

Alex Salmond's new Arbroath 'declaration of opportunity' suggested that only through independence would the NHS avoid 'privatisation and fragmentation'. David Cameron countered by pointing out that health is a devolved matter and that only the Scottish First Minister could privatise.[93]

Danny Alexander meanwhile said there was 'absolutely nothing' that Salmond could do to ensure that an independent Scotland could have a currency union.[94] A panel-based poll indicated that such statements make 28 per cent more likely to vote Yes and 25 per cent more likely to vote No.[95]

Polly Toynbee comes out for sustaining the Union in her *Guardian* column, as it will increase the chances of a social democratic Britain in the future – 'A community of people bound by broad values is far more inspiring to me than small groups of people dividing up particular pieces of turf.'[96]

The Secretary General of Nato, Anders Fogh Rasmussen, has said again that an independent Scotland wouldn't automatically slip into the organisation.[97] *The Times* runs an intriguing poll which indicates that '45 per cent of Scots think that Mr Salmond is the wrong man to lead the Yes campaign. Only a third of voters think he was the right choice'.[98] The perils of overexposure – of being the most dazzling show in town for too long; palate fatigue on the part of the electorate with a star turn who has become overfamiliar and predictable?

Did a long interview with STV this afternoon in which I was asked what trace AS would leave on history if it's a No. I said a very considerable one – a man who had a force around him.

## Wednesday 20 August 2014

A surprising – and pleasing – statistic this morning. A 'Future of England Survey' (part of Richard Wyn Jones's work at Cardiff) has found that 59 per cent of the English want Scotland to stay with the UK and 19 per cent favour separation. It's a higher proportion wishing for Union than I would have expected.

But the survey shows it's conditional love. For a start only 23 per cent think an independent Scotland should be allowed to share the pound. Only 26 per cent believe the remainder of the UK should help an independent Scotland join the EU and Nato. Only 10 per cent believe a Scottish separation would improve relations between the two countries. Unsurprisingly, if we stay together, 56 per cent thought the public spending bounty of the Barnett Formula should be stopped and 63 per cent want Scottish MPs to be prevented from voting on English legislation.[99]

## Thursday 21 August 2014

Have been looking at the figures on which yesterday's stories about English opinion were based. YouGov did the polling in April. The researchers rightly emphasise that: 'The views of English voters are not only starkly at odds with those of the Scottish Government regarding what should follow from a Yes vote. They also contradict the Unionist parties about what should be the consequences of a No victory' not least on sustaining the Barnett formula. And the researchers highlight the response that worries me greatly – the possibility of a creeping estrangement after a No vote:

> Voters in England are also inclined to be pessimistic about the future of the union even after a No vote in Scotland. Some 37% agreed with the proposition that even after a No vote, 'Scotland and England will continue to drift apart', whereas only 21% disagreed.[100]

Tim Montgomerie made clever use of the data in yesterday's *Times* arguing that 'if the battle for Scotland is nearly over, the battle for England might be about to begin'. After reprising the English survey's findings he wrote:

> Until now the Conservatives haven't felt it necessary to respond to the English awakening. It is not, after all, in the interests of Mr Miliband or Mr Clegg to empower an England leaning to the right. But I know a man who

would benefit from tickling England's tummy. He smokes. He drinks pints. And he's called Nigel. He's got nothing to lose in wrapping himself in the St George's Cross and I predict he will.[101]

I shall be very surprised if he doesn't.

The more I think about it, there's going to be a huge amount of repair work needed by the Union from 19 September on. We will not be the same the other side of that vote.

Today oil and gas have seeped back into the Scottish question. Sir Ian Wood, who prepared the 2012 review for the Westminster government on oil and gas recovery and regulation, has given an interview claiming the Scottish government is substantially overestimating future flows. He said the SNP government's estimate of a further 24 billion barrels left in the North Sea was between 45 and 65 per cent too high and that their £7 billion figure for tax revenue was £2 billion too much. He spoke particularly to the younger voters in Scotland in his interview with *Energy Voice* reported in *The Times*:

> Long term, we will not have significant oil and gas reserves and that will have an impact, so young voters right now should just be aware that by the time they are middle-aged they will begin to see a real run-down, not just in the level of oil and gas being produced, but in all the ongoing implications of that – the jobs, the economic prosperity, public services – and that run-down will begin in 2030, only 15 years away.

His conclusion? 'Everything I looked at ... suggests that, with one or two exceptions, the best of both worlds is clearly the right way ahead.'[102] Alistair will fashion that assessment into a rapier in Monday night's debate, I reckon.

### Sunday 24 August 2014

On the theme of the Union needing repair post-19 September, *The Independent on Sunday* carries an intriguing ComRes poll which asked unusual questions: 'In Scotland, 65 per cent said they felt favourable towards the English – whereas in England and Wales only 52 per cent said the same about the Scots.' On independence itself, 12 per cent were favourable to it in England and Wales compared to 45 per cent in Scotland.[103]

Meanwhile, Danny Alexander has weighed in behind Ian Wood's analysis of oil and gas prospects.[104]

Crucial week coming up. Second and last Salmond v Darling on Monday evening. Then on Tuesday and Wednesday 700,000 postal votes go out across Scotland, almost a fifth of the electorate. A proportion of them, no doubt, will fill in their preference fairly swiftly.[105]

### Monday 25 August 2014

Great Debate Day No.2. Caught snatches of Jim Naughtie's discussion on *Today* this morning after a very damp Bank Holiday walk. Jim reflected the heat of the final weeks of, as he said, a two- or even three-year campaign. He also pointed out that Yes had expected to be ahead in the polls by this stage (the gap still seems to be 14% between No and Yes).

Much trailing in the papers of Salmond's intention to go

hard on the NHS. The briefing seems to be that AS was too conversational and moderate in Debate 1 as part of his wooing of the undecided and that tonight will be the moment for a negative, fear-inducing alternative, with the spectre of a Conservative government in Westminster post the 2015 election. Alistair is expected to go strong on oil and gas and an independent Scotland's inability to walk into the EU.

Maybe the UK-wide screening of tonight's debate on BBC2 will wake up the English a bit more as to the magnitude of the decision. (Debate 1 was on STV which only went to Scotland and the wider streaming arrangement broke down.)

Salmond will do better tonight than last time and the expectations of Darling are much higher – so does the political market make its adjustments.

*The Times* juxtaposes stories on both the Scottish question[106] and the European question – reflecting steers that at the Conservative Party Conference David Cameron is preparing to raise the spectre of Britain leaving the European Union should it reject a large overhaul of its rules.[107]

Reminds me of my own catastrophe theory – or catastrophe scenario, to be exact – which has been bothering me since the spring, when one of the most thoughtful people in Whitehall painted it for me over lunch. It runs like this:

**September 2014.** Scotland votes to stay part of the United Kingdom. The polls and surveys suggest that economic factors were the main determinants of the outcome.

**June 2017 (or by the end of the decade).** The UK as a whole votes in a referendum to leave the European Union (probably by a narrowish margin). The figures show that Scotland, however, voted to remain part of the EU. In the aftermath, and while the Brexit negotiations get under way, opinion in Scotland, in effect, says the September 2014 deal is off. The economic unit we voted to remain part of is about to be fundamentally changed; no automatic access to the European Single Market and much else. We would like another referendum. It would be very hard for Westminster/Whitehall to resist this demand and unwise to. So …

**September 2022 or 2023.** Scotland votes in a referendum to leave the UK leaving, I fear, the Remainder of the UK (as Whitehall calls it) a shrivelled, inward-looking nation which is poorer in both its material and non-material dimensions and much reduced in its place in the world.

That for me would be a catastrophe – and it's perfectly possible within a decade.

Heaven forbid that the next 24 days produce a late, referendum-winning surge for the Yes vote, starting the countdown to a shrivelled RUK outside Europe and trying to make its way in the cold Northern seas as a kind of Singapore on the Atlantic Rim.

**Tuesday 26 August 2014**
Last night's debate was a lowering experience and occasionally painful to watch. Alistair Darling was nervous and off-form. Alex Salmond was back on form with his trademark populism and the sometimes sneering partisanship which I've long felt diminishes this gifted man.

Glenn Campbell, the BBC's moderator, put in one or two good, sharp questions but he allowed the mutual interrogation section to get utterly out of hand with both men, voices raised, speaking over each other.

From the opening statements one could tell Salmond was back ('Much more animated than last time', I wrote on my notepad) and that Darling was not firing in the way he eventually did in the earlier debate. He made his points on the currency, the economy, oil and public spending well but there was no bite to it. And he gathered neither pace nor penetration as time passed.

Salmond, as Jim Naughtie noted on the *Today* programme this morning, played to the West of Scotland Labour vote (health, poverty, Trident – though on Faslane an impressive chunky questioner pushed him hard on job losses and the First Minister's response that an independent Scotland would have its defence headquarters there and create new jobs to fill the gap was unconvincing).

It was a scrappy, noisy affair. The Salmond supporters in the Kelvingrove Gallery and Museum out-clapped and out-heckled the Better Together people. A sharp, post-debate ICM poll for *The Guardian* gave the palm to Salmond – 71% to Darling's 29% – and across the papers the headlines this morning declare Salmond the winner.

But will it make any difference? That same ICM poll, as *The Guardian* puts it, 'also suggested that Salmond's victory in the BBC debate ... made little difference to the overall levels of support for independence'.[108]

Tam Dalyell rang again this morning just before nine and was pretty gloomy. Though Salmond had evaded the big questions, Tam thought Alistair had not performed well. He thought Darling had been 'holed below the water-line' by Salmond's pushing him on what extra powers devo-max would bring. Tam took some comfort from what the BBC's Alan Little said on the 10 o'clock news about how it's the discussions within families that matter, not what people say on television. 'I think and hope he's right,' says Tam.[109]

It does look as if the key battleground is the West of Scotland Labour vote. Tommy McAvoy [Labour frontbencher in the House of Lords] was very interesting about this when we chatted a couple of months ago. Tommy said traditionally the West of Scotland Catholic Labour vote had been solid for the Union for fear of a Parliament in Edinburgh becoming a Scottish Stormont. But with 15 years of experience of Holyrood and no sign of that these anxieties have disappeared. Tommy was worried, too, about the Orange Lodges wishing to march with the Better Togethers. Tam, too, is concerned about the big pro-Union Orange Lodge marches planned for Edinburgh on the Saturday before the poll.

There was a flash of cheer in last night's debate towards the end, when both Salmond and Darling stressed the need for Scotland to come together after the vote. Salmond even offered Darling a place on the negotiating team after a Yes vote. This also impressed Mike White in *The Guardian*: 'Nice one, Alex. Better than last time. But no knockout punch.'[110]

Also, in his concluding statement, Alistair stressed Scotland's huge contribution to the UK and the world since the Enlightenment out of all proportion to its size – but he didn't make it ring or sing. Peculiar thing, politics – what appeared to be his strengths in the first debate seem to those polled by ICM to have come over as a handicap last night. Though Darling, for me, produced the best single line – 'We do not need to divide these islands into separate states to assert our Scottish identity.' I await the next batch of polls with a touch (though no more than that) of trepidation.

## Thursday 28 August 2014

The EU Brexit question has come alive within the Scotland debate. One hundred and fifty Scottish businessmen and women pro Yes have come out in retaliation[111] against yesterday's 130 business Nos.[112] In so doing they make the point about how a still together Scotland would suffer if the UK withdrew from the EU.

The powerful Peter Sutherland, with the force of a former Director-General of the World Trade Organisation, EU Commissioner for Trade and Chairman of BP, has an op-ed piece in this morning's *Guardian*. 'Scotland', he says 'is the strongest base of pro-European sentiment in the UK'. Peter finished his piece with what he rightly sees as a certainty – 'if Scotland votes for independence in September, a referendum within the rump UK on continued EU membership would be even less likely to produce a victory for those who remain'.[113]

David Cameron will be talking to the Scottish CBI today and urging Scotland not to abandon one of the 'oldest and most successful single markets in the world' (i.e. the UK). Teresa May was in Scotland yesterday stressing the intelligence and security price of separation: 'We spend some £33bn a year on defence, and over £2bn a year for the security and intelligence agencies and National Cyber Security Programme. An independent Scotland would not be able to share these agencies. It would have to build its own infra-structure – and pick up the bill.'[114]

## Friday 29 August 2014

The European Question has shot back like a jolt of elec-tricity with Douglas Carswell's defection yesterday to UKIP and the by-election he has precipitated in Clacton some time in October. The press is full of speculation about the number of Conservative MPs who might do the same if Carswell is returned. Tough day for David Cameron. Appar-ently the Carswell defection took him and everyone else by surprise as he was on his way to Glasgow for the Scottish CBI dinner.[115]

Tough in a different way for Labour's Jim Murphy, a good and decent man, who yesterday was in Kirkcaldy on the 79th day of his '100 streets' tour of Scotland. Attempts were made to shout him down, he was pelted with eggs and a lady on a mobility scooter got to the front and tried to grab his micro-phone. Apparently he's faced trouble elsewhere: in Mother-well his tables of campaign literature were overturned. Mike Wade's report in *The Times* on Jim's travails has produced the most bizarre sentence of the referendum coverage so far: 'In Oban, the local "gull whisperer" is said to have summoned the birds to defecate on Mr Murphy's head.'[116]

I shall have to have a go at that next time I'm in Orkney.

*The Times* reports Jim Murphy as saying the mood is growing uglier by the day: 'I thought this was meant to be the brave new politics. The nearer the decision gets, the worse it's getting. I don't know what they will do with their misplaced aggression if they lose.'

A *Daily Mail*/Survation poll suggests it's getting closer. 53% No; 47% Yes (though Survation is the poll that's shown higher figures for Yes than the others).

Alistair Carmichael has said something interesting – that he had been considering his future if it's a Yes: 'If Scotland votes for independence then I would still want to be part of Scottish public political life. I would have to be realistic about what could be achieved, but you know I am not walking away from Scottish politics.'[117]

As if to add to David Cameron's difficulties, at the Glasgow Dinner the CBI President, Sir Mike Rake, brought the focus back to European uncertainties: 'We accept that calling a referendum on EU membership is a constitutional issue for government, but the ambiguity has already, and is increasingly, causing real concern for business regarding their future investment.'[118]

What a troubled kingdom we are, with the Scottish Question and the European Question intermingling like a couple of turbulent weather systems.

### Monday 1 September 2014

The venom seeping from parts of the campaign is coming out. Jim Murphy suspended his 100 streets tour on Friday for 72 hours so that he could consult the police. Jim said: 'What we have discovered is that there is a dark corner in Scotland in which lurks a kind of noisy, intolerant nationalism that has now been brought to life and co-ordinated in Facebook postings and elsewhere through Yes Scotland.'

Yes Scotland have condemned 'abusive, dangerous and offensive behaviour'. Asked about the eggs hurled at Jim

Murphy, *The Times* reported Alex Salmond as saying, 'I don't think it's at the serious end of things, but it shouldn't happen' and he let it be known that he had been subjected to dangerous tail-gating road rage by a motorist.[119]

I think what's happened to Jim Murphy *is* 'at the serious end of things'. When we talked on the phone last night, Tam Dalyell described it as 'stinking'. Kathleen Dalyell is very worried about both the possible outcome and the country after a Yes: 'I just think it will be a nasty Scotland; inward looking. And if they don't get into Europe or the currency they want they'll say it's England's fault.'

Spent the weekend in Norfolk with Gillian and Tom Shephard. Gill has always been anxious about the outcome of the referendum, fearing a late surge towards yes.

Salmond did not rise to the level of events in a television interview yesterday. He condemned all the 'odd idiots' on both sides who caused such problems, then, as is his style, he could not resist qualifying that in a way that sneers at his opponents: 'I don't hold press conferences accusing Mr Murphy or the No campaign of orchestrating these events because I know it would be ridiculous to do so.'[120]

Magnus Linklater has a characteristically thoughtful piece in *The Times* op-ed. He concludes in a justifiably sombre fashion:

The great majority of the Yes supporters are just as repelled by the threats and intimidation as their opponents. Vociferous as the cybernats are, they represent an outer fringe, and though Mr Salmond could do a great deal more to call them off, there's no evidence that he's encouraging them. The fear is, however, that when the outcome is decided – whichever way the vote goes – deep divisions will be exposed. The ferocity of the tactics has opened up wounds within Scotland. These will be hard to heal.[121]

Talked to Kevin Tebbit [former Permanent Secretary at the Ministry of Defence] on the phone this morning. Kev fears that 'whatever happens, politics is going to be very nasty', in the coming months (he was thinking of UKIP, too).

John Curtice's latest assessment is that the 'leadership debates have made very little if any difference to the balance of opinion in the referendum race'.[122] John's poll-of-polls, taken over the period 4–28, August suggests the running is 56% No; 44% Yes.[123]

## Tuesday 2 September 2014

Drop into my newsagent's on Orford Road, Walthamstow on the way back from my walk this shiny, fresh September morning and there it is. Bam! The headline which part of me had been fearing, above *The Times's* splash on its front page:

Scotland poll puts Union on knife-edge

No calm, detached analysis for me on the way home. It's as if the United Kingdom that made me is about to be flung into the air to fall in fragments. I can't bear the thought that this pamphlet might turn into a personal epitaph for an extraordinary UK that has done great things together, with heaps more things to do.

YouGov says its 53 No, 47 Yes, with undecided voters

twice as likely to break for independence if they vote on 18 September. Peter Kellner of YouGov tells *The Times*: 'A close finish looks likely and a Yes victory is now a real possibility. If No finally wins the day, it now looks less likely that it will win by a big enough margin to deliver a knock-out blow to supporters of independence. If the final vote is anything like our current figures, I would not bet much against a second referendum being held within the next 10 to 15 years.'[124]

I've written this down as soon as I reached home. No doubt, I'll calm down a bit later.

I read Magnus Linklater's analysis of the YouGov findings and draw what solace I can from his final paragraph:

> There are ... 16 vital days to go. Referendums are notoriously hard to predict and anything can happen in that final, frenetic period. This latest poll offers supporters of the Union one huge advantage. It finally blasts aside the lingering fog of complacency. The fight is on. And there is no time to lose.[125]

Now after breakfast and a bath, a modicum of calm has returned. My instinct is that it will go the No way on 18 September but not by the margin I was predicting last month – that it will be Together By A Thread or TBAT. TBAT will bring considerable problems and lead to a perpetual campaign of the one-more-heave variety until the next time, with the creeping estrangement I've always feared becoming increasingly palpable.

Meanwhile Putin is exercising increasing pressure on Ukraine, ISIS is brutalising swathes of Syria and Iraq – and

John Bercow is struggling to find a way out of the hole he has dug on the path to finding a successor to the great Sir Robert Rogers as Clerk of the House of Commons. What a time for us to be teetering on the edge of sundering our country.

Pessimism rampant? Not really. We are after all, the 59th-Minute-of-the-Eleventh-Hour nation – waking up with seconds to spare to perilous realities. Or am I, as is my custom, falling once more into what David Runciman calls the 'confidence trap?'

## Wednesday 3 September 2014

Yesterday's poll sent a pulse through the financial and currency markets. Bill O'Neill of UBS is reported in the *FT* as saying a Yes vote would face investors with 'unfathomable levels of uncertainty'.

The *FT* said: 'The most pronounced reaction was in currency options markets: the cost of buying protection against swings in the pound around the date of the vote rose as companies and speculators sought to hedge their risks.'

Lloyds let it be known that it had prepared contingency plans to move its head office from Edinburgh to London in the event of a Yes.[126]

The House of Commons is back, so MPs on the Treasury Select Committee had a chance to question Nick Macpherson [Permanent Secretary to the Treasury] about HMG's contingency planning – or lack of – for the consequences of a Yes. They triggered a classic Nickism:

> There are plans and plans. We may have made contingency plans about contingency plans, by which I mean if

Scotland were to vote for independence in the early hours of the morning ... we will have a team in place tasked with dealing with this.[127]

The pound fell by 0.7% against the dollar and 0.6% against the Euro yesterday, with currency dealers warning of further falls between now and 18 September.

Ollie Rehn, the former EU Commissioner for monetary matters, said in a letter to Danny Alexander that an independent Scotland could not join the EU unless it had a central bank – that 'sterlingisation', using the pound outside a currency union with the remainder of the UK, would not work.[128]

*The Times* runs a sombre YouGov UK-wide poll showing that 50% believe 'The country will be left divided' if there's a Yes vote and 54% believing the same if there's a No.[129]

Jim Murphy, I'm glad to say, was back on the road yesterday on the Mound in Edinburgh and the nasties stayed away. 'Whoever turned on that noisy tap of aggressive political behaviour has quietly turned it off again.' Standing on his Irn Bru crates, he told his listeners that Scotland was 'a cantankerous nation' that had achieved so much. 'We can still shape the world together. How does it help for Scotland to walk away from a seat on the UN Security Council, from the G8, from the EU?'[130]

Alex Salmond said yesterday he was still the underdog but Scotland was in the grip of a 'democratic sensation'.[131] Scotland may be electrified but it's spooking the money markets. Now that the jolt has woken them up they'll stay jumpy at least until the small hours of Friday 19 September.

## Thursday 4 September 2014

Goldman Sachs came out yesterday with stark warnings about the immediate consequences of separation, indicating that the Bank of England might have to intervene to support the pound within hours of a Yes vote. Kevin Daly, a senior economist at Goldman, predicted 'severe consequences' for both Scotland and the rest of the UK: 'Even if the sterling monetary union does not break up in the event of a Yes vote, the threat of a break-up would provide investors with a strong incentive to sell Scottish-based assets, and householders with a strong incentive to withdraw deposits from Scottish-based banks.' So a run on the pound and a run on the Scottish banks which would take shoring up by the Bank of England. Daly said the B of E would probably have to commit itself to propping up the Scottish banks throughout the separation negotiations.[132]

It all underscores the testing novelty of what we would face post a Yes vote. How do you sunder a kingdom? We reached some 40 independence settlements with former imperial possessions between India in 1947 and Zimbabwe in 1980. But this is quite a different prospect. Three hundred and seven years of political and economic union within a United Kingdom would make it a rending like no other we have experienced – a tearing out of flesh of our flesh.

Tuesday's YouGov poll has stimulated a rash of speculation about the immediate consequences of sundering. Some of his own MPs are urging David Cameron, post-Yes, to rush through a statute postponing the May 2015 election for a year so that Labour would not have the benefit of its Scottish MPs.[133] Not a runner. Postponing elections during the two

total wars of the twentieth century was necessary and justi-
fied. This would not be. Such a suggestion also assumes that
separation day could be reached as soon as March 2016, as
Salmond wishes. An unrealistic prospect. (Andrew Turnbull
[the former Cabinet Secretary] had a nice line on this yesterday when we talked: 'He who has the shortest deadline needs
the deepest pocket.')

We'll have another poll by the end of the week. Can't
remember when one carried such freight of hope/anxiety
depending on where you stand.

Just two weeks to go.

## Friday 5 September 2014

Tam Dalyell on the phone this morning was both gloomy
and fuming. He and Kathleen think the position is 'dire ...
I'm really in despair'.

Tam thinks both Cameron and Miliband made matters
worse yesterday. The PM said on the *Today* programme that
separation would break his heart. 'A lot of people reacted
by saying, "Let's break Cameron's heart". Ed Miliband was
bloody stupid. To come and attack the Tories in Scotland at
this stage was ludicrous. Just think of the effect on the Tories
inside the Better Together campaign. Once it's thought
there's dissension within Better Together ... I can't contain
my anger with Miliband'. Tam wondered who on earth was
advising Miliband in his office.

'Do you think it might happen?'

'It looks as if it might happen', replied Tam. 'Yes I feel
in the position of Cassandra. Thirty-five years ago I wrote
*Devolution: The End of Britain*. No-one believed me. Like

Cassandra, I wasn't listened to except by Hugh Trevor-Roper who wrote the Foreword. They don't understand that Scotland will become a foreign country.' Tam thinks independence will mean border controls – frontiers – because of the difference in immigration policies North and South.

Ed Miliband, after what appears to have been a rather bleak – and heckled – walkabout in Keir Hardie country, addressed a meeting in Blantyre. His line was that Scotland could only become a just and fairer society if they voted No this month and for Labour next May.[134]

Both the PM and Ed said yesterday they would not resign their leaderships if it's a Yes. *The Independent* picks up noises I'd heard at Westminster this week that a Yes could lead to a leadership challenge to Cameron. An unnamed former Conservative minister is quoted as saying: 'Losing Scotland would be a traumatic event, a horror show that David Cameron could not possibly survive.' A senior Tory MP is cited as predicting: 'The move will take place immediately.'[135]

I've been having a number of nuclear conversations this week for various reasons. There's still no contingency planning happening on Faslane/Coulport. Alex Salmond's claim that the moving of nuclear weapons would need no more than five years is an absurd underestimate. To replicate the base somewhere in the remainder of the UK would take 20 years and an extra £20 billion to the cost of keeping ourselves a nuclear-weapons state.

Devonport isn't a runner. The Vanguards are too heavy to get in for their refits unless all the missiles are taken out. Can you store warheads anywhere there?

Falmouth. Possible. But think of the local resistance.

Planning laws have got far tighter since the 1960s and the Government would have to take special powers of some kind. Ditto Milford Haven. Some parts of the oil storage facilities have gone but there's still heaps of gas. Would it be wise to place it in a devolved country with an Assembly that would almost certainly be opposed to the move? Could you persuade naval families to settle there? It would take a great quantity of national political will to do it, as well as much time and money. It could give a future Labour Cabinet the let-out that some of its members would be pleased to take ('We'd like to have carried on – but it's too big an ask').

What about the interim period if every sinew *was* devoted to carrying on? The boats could use King's Bay, Georgia in the US. But could the UK warheads be stored there too? Knowledgeable people are divided on whether the 1968 Non Proliferation Treaty would allow it, as such storage is not 'historic', i.e. pre-1968. Others think it would be all right if the D5 warheads were under 'national', i.e. Royal Navy, control in the King's Bay facility.

MoD is *sans* plans, *sans* costed options on any of these things.

On the security front, John Scarlett has a powerful op-ed piece in today's *Times* writing as a former 'C' who comes from a Scots family. He steers clear of the 'Five Eyes' alliance [the intelligence-pooling arrangement between the US, the UK, Canada, Australia and New Zealand], but makes vivid the difficulty any separate Scottish secret service would face in coming anywhere near what the UK intelligence community can provide.[136] I'm surprised – but pleased – that he's written the piece.

**Sunday 7 September 2014**

This is the weekend the Union stared into the abyss. YouGov, polling for *The Sunday Times*, has Yes on 51%; No on 49%.[137]

A 22% No lead has been overturned in a month. YouGov suggests 35% of Labour voters will now vote Yes. The West of Scotland Labour heartlands have shifted. If they continue to do so, that's it.

An abyss can be a profound stimulant to second thoughts and a surge of 'Are we sure about this?' If it isn't, the impact will be immense and long-lasting. By comparison the breaking up of the remaining Empire in the 1960s will look like a historical pimple that caused scarcely a rash of irritation in the home islands.

The psychological mood has shifted, too. The UK has really woken up this week thanks to the YouGov polls. Much attention is being paid to the aftermath in terms of Westminster politics (can Cameron and Miliband survive a break-up of the Union on their watches). And the Palace factor is seeping in.

*The Sunday Times* double-decker splash headline reflects this:

Yes leads in Scots poll shock
'Unionist' Queen fears break-up of UK

Beneath is a picture of HMQ and Prince Charles looking very sombre at the Braemar Games. The PM is flying up to see the Queen today (premiers always visit Balmoral at some point in September; but none has ever arrived, in peacetime, against such a backdrop of anxiety).

*The Sunday Times* runs the Palace factor through its main story:

> [The YouGov poll] comes as Buckingham Palace aides revealed that the Queen has a 'great deal of concern' about the prospect of Scotland breaking away and has asked for daily updates on the progress of the campaign.
>
> While Palace officials say the Queen is neutral over the referendum, a senior royal source claimed: 'The Queen is a unionist ... There is now a great deal of concern'.
>
> Senior aides are worried that she will be pitched into a constitutional crisis that threatens her status as Scottish head of state and her oath to uphold the Church of Scotland. 'If there is a "Yes" vote, that puts us into uncharted territory constitutionally', one aide said. 'Nothing is certain. Her being Queen of Scotland is not a given.'

## Monday 8 September 2014

There is an air of desperation about the last 10 days. In the next day or so, HMG – with Labour and Lib Dem agreement – are going to lay out a parliamentary timetable for what will essentially be devo-max if we stay together.[138]

The money markets don't like it either. The papers predicted this morning that sterling would fall.[139] It duly did. At 4pm it was down to $1.61, its lowest against the dollar for 10 months.

Two opinion polls and the kingdom and the currency rock. And so have I (rocked, that is). It's not pleasant living on the rim. It's hard to think about anything else. Even if it *is* all right on the day, the past six days since the first YouGov have administered one helluva shock.

John Curtice pointed out yesterday that Panelbase, 'hitherto the company that consistently produced the most optimistic picture for Yes', still think No are trailing 48% to 52%. It's the level of delusion that's really worrying me. As John Curtice reported yesterday:

> *More voters than ever* – 51% – now say that the No side is bluffing when it claims that the rest of the UK would not allow Scotland to share the pound in a monetary union. This figure is now 12 points higher than it was after the *initial currency intervention* [by George Osborne and the Treasury] in February. The decline in the credibility of the No campaign in voters' eyes is also replicated by the finding that rather more voters (46%) now think the *Yes campaign is honest* than say the same of the *No campaign* (40%), a reversal of the position when the question was first asked in June.[140]

Martin Kettle captures the living-on-the-rim feeling perfectly in his opinion piece on the front page of this morning's *Guardian*. Why has it taken the rest of us so long to realise Scotland is a first-order question?

Here's Martin this morning:

> With only 10 days to go, the rest of Britain finally awoke yesterday to the enormity of what is happening in Scotland. For years, the rise of Scottish national feeling has been underestimated and misunderstood. The possibility that the United Kingdom might be heading for the history books has been complacently dismissed as unthinkable. But there can be no excuse for any ignorance or complacency now.

This weekend the unthinkable has elbowed its way into the driving seat of the Scottish campaign. No other issue now matters in British politics. These may not be 10 days that will shake the world, as John Reed called the Russian revolution. But they will be 10 days that could change all our lives, shaking the British state, and its people to their very foundations.[141]

Tristan Garel-Jones [a former Conservative minister] tells me this afternoon that Better Together have missed a trick by failing to point out that 'the bloody Celts have been running the show' in Whitehall and Westminster with all those PMs, Cabinet Ministers and Permanent Secretaries.

On the HMQ front, the Palace spokesman, very properly said this:

> The referendum is a matter for the people of Scotland: the Queen remains strictly neutral on this, as she does on all political issues. The Queen has maintained a close interest in the referendum, as she does with all major matters of public debate, and is being kept informed by her ministers and officials in the usual way.

The YouGov poll brought out the substantial streak of republicanism in the Yes camp. 46% of them believe an independent Scotland should break its links with the monarchy.[142] Radio 4's *World At One* were after me to follow this up. I suggested they dig out their recording of the Queen's words to both Houses of Parliament in 1977. They have.

**Tuesday 9 September 2014**

A slightly bonkers day of near-perpetual radio and television interviews. The Scottish electricity has really surged south. Westminsters and the broadcasters are speaking of little else (quite rightly).

This morning's papers are fuelled by three factors – the pound falling yesterday by 1 per cent plus Scotland's FTSE companies losing £2.6bn between them; Gordon Brown leading off on devo-max in a speech in a Midlothian Miners' Institute and Cameron, Miliband and Clegg following in his wake; *The Daily Telegraph* reporting senior Tories urging the Queen to say something (which she can't).[143]

The recording of HMQ's Westminster Hall speech in 1977 is the trigger for my interview with James Robbins on the *World at One* this lunchtime.

People are really waking up to what it means. Gill Shephard told me on the phone last night she thought it was lost already: 'I think reason has left ... I just think it's unstoppable'. Maurice Glasman the Labour peer told me the same on the Terrace at lunchtime. He's prepared a pamphlet called 'Rediscovering England' in case separation happens.

Snatched a quick chat this morning with Bob Maclennan who is close to despair: 'It's an absolute nightmare. The break-up of Great Britain. I'm feeling very emotional at the moment. How did we get to this point?'

Bob thinks because the prospect was not taken seriously enough by the party leaders down here. Clegg, Darling and Douglas Alexander thought his idea of an all-UK convention was a good idea – but nothing happened.

My assessment? We'll stay together. Just. People will pause in the polling booth and say: 'Are we sure?'

PMQs have been cancelled for tomorrow so that the three party leaders can rush north.

Gordon Brown laid out a very swift timetable leading to a fusing of the three parties' ideas and a devo-max White Paper. A declaration of intent is fine. But it shouldn't be rushed. Constitutional statues need carefully constructing if they are to (a) endure and (b) fit with other moving parts of the constitution.

I hear that No.10 is truly shaken by all this. My clever political journo friends do think Cameron would have to resign if it's separation.

## Wednesday 10 September 2014

Just watched the 7pm news on BBC News 24. The *Daily Record* tomorrow has a Survation poll indicating 53% No; 47% Yes; 10% undecided. Its poll of polls is running at 52–48. A dash of (deeply qualified) temporary relief. At least it looks as if there isn't an avalanche underway towards Yes.

Did still more interviews today. Said on the BBC World Service that the YouGov polls had sent 'an electromagnetic pulse' south from Scotland which has shocked us into a greater sense of reality and possibility.

Jim Naughtie said on *Today* this morning that No could pay a high cost if any of the party leaders put a foot wrong in Scotland today. As far as I can judge from the television reports, they haven't. David Cameron got quite emotional during his speech in the financial district. There was a catch in his voice as he said: 'We care passionately about this family of nations. And we would be desperately sad if it was torn apart.'

Standard Life has confirmed it will send its pensions and savings down south if it's a Yes. Mark Carney told the Commons Treasury Committee the Bank have contingency plans to ensure everyone's accounts are safe north and south of the border if it's a Yes. Bob Dudley has said it's better for BP if its offshore operations continue to be conducted on a UK basis.

*The Times* led this morning on the Palace squashing the Queen-should-intervene story. HMQ's spokesman, 'In unusually forceful language which betrayed signs of irritation at the highest level', expressed it thus:

> The sovereign's constitutional impartiality is an established principle of our democracy and one which the Queen has demonstrated throughout her reign. As such, the monarch is above politics and those in political office have a duty to ensure that this remains the case. Any suggestion that the Queen would wish to influence the outcome of the current referendum campaign is categorically wrong. Her Majesty is firmly of the view that this is a matter for the people of Scotland.[144]

The good Sir Christopher Geidt wields a strong pen and a firm vocabulary.

*The Times* names Henry Bellingham on the Conservative side and Simon Danczuk on Labour's as among the MPs urging the Queen to say something.

### Friday 12 September 2014
It's Friday evening. By this time next week we'll be a different country. If it's a vote for separation, *very* different.

As today's *Economist* put it in its first leader, 'UK RIP?'

This great multinational state could be undone in a single day, by a poll in which just 19% of its citizens will participate. That outcome, once unthinkable, would be bad for Scotland and tragic for what remained of the UK.[145]

I still think we will be intact as a kingdom – just.

YouGov in this morning's *Times* suggests it coming slowly back to a No (52% to 48%) with women and the young moving towards Better Together.[146]

So, where are we after a week in which Whitehall, in the words of a well-placed insider, reached 'near panic'?

The banks and big companies have been queuing up to warn.[147] Alex Salmond got ratty, especially with Nick Robinson, at yesterday's international press conference.[148]

I was over at ITN in Millbank yesterday afternoon prerecording for next Friday (on the two outcomes) and suggested to the chums that there were multiple conspiracies building for the more inflamed and embittered nationalists to wheel out if they lost (Treasury and Bank winding up international capital and all that) only to be told that Salmond had already done a bit of this claiming that the Treasury had leaked RBS re-headquartering plans to the BBC.

A worry that I'm reluctant to commit to paper. That by this time next week disturbances might have broken out in one or two places in Scotland if it's a No vote. I would be very surprised if Police Scotland did not have contingency plans in place for exactly this.

A touch of light relief yesterday afternoon. Met Frank

Field, one of my oldest and most cherished Labour friends, in the Westminster tube station:

> PH: Are you worried about next week?
> FF: No I'm not. The sooner we can get them off our nipples, the sooner we can work on a new English identity.

On Wednesday *FT's* Public Policy Editor, Sarah Neville, rang me to ask how 'the Establishment' was taking the uncertainty. The result appeared this morning under the headline:

Ruling elite aghast as union wobbles

It seems I am a member of said 'ruling elite' (not quite how I see myself). I talk of the 'electro-magnetic pulse' that has belatedly woken up what Sarah calls 'the UK's political and administrative classes'. I then bang on a bit about the absence of contingency planning and Sarah builds her last paragraph on my thoughts about sundering:

> For Lord Hennessy, any dismembering of the UK will take Britain into territory for which it remains utterly unready, for all its past experience in colonial handovers. 'This is not the extended family, as the empire used to be called, it is the immediate family', he said. 'This is flesh of our flesh. It is not severance in an "imperial disposal" way; it is rending'.[149]

So it will be by this time next week if it's a Yes.

## Saturday 13 September 2014

The electromagnetic pulse continues to send down shock-waves from the north. The ICM poll in this morning's *Guardian* has it on 51% No, 49% Yes.[150]

August's figures, released yesterday, showed that nearly £17 billion of shares, bonds and assets poured out of the UK as a whole last month.[151]

Mark Carney will return from next week's G8 early. George Osborne won't go at all.[152]

A picket boat full of former First Sea Lords has warned in a letter to the *Telegraph* of the consequences in jobs, investment and overall security if we separate – that breaking up the UK's Armed Forces 'could lead to the loss of premier-league capability for ever'.[153]

A whole string of economists have warned of severe consequences for Scotland in particular but also for the remainder of the UK if we split – from the chief economist of Deutsche Bank, David Folkerts-Landau, saying it would be a mistake on a par with Churchill as Chancellor of the Exchequer in 1925 taking us back to the gold standard, to Larry Summers, the former US Treasury Secretary, talking of 'very grave consequences that would follow' a Yes, hoping Scots 'will cast a vote for the future rather than a vote of frustration'.[154]

Meanwhile Jim Sillars, Alex Salmond's former deputy (the two are now reconciled after falling out), has poured flames on the fire and sketched the we-wuz-robbed/conspiracy theory that might rise from the ashes of a Yes camp defeat. This what he said yesterday:

This referendum is about power, and when we get a Yes

majority, we use that power for a day of reckoning with BP and the banks.

The heads of these companies are rich men, in cahoots with a rich English Tory Prime Minister, to keep Scotland's poor poorer, through lies and distortions. The power they have now to subvert our democracy will come to an end with a Yes.

He went on to say that BP would have to 'learn the meaning of nationalisation' and if it wanted access to 'monster fields' of oil west of Shetland 'it will have to learn to bend the knee to a greater power – us, the sovereign people of Scotland'. For good measure, Jim Sillars wants a boycott of John Lewis stores.[155]

The markets will inhale this stuff and react accordingly, thus fuelling still further Mr Sillars's conspiracy theory which, I fear, may become a conventional wisdom in certain minds in Scotland if we stay together.

It's going to be a rough week in the markets and for many a nervous system on both sides of the argument. The electromagnetic pulse is now reaching the wider world. On Thursday the *FT* reported that: 'Economic officials in Washington have only just woken up to the chances of a Yes vote ...' On Wednesday the IMF warned of consequential market turbulence.[156]

This is really shaping up into a crisis that's got the lot – currency, constitution, place-in-the-world and individual and party political fortunes both north and south of the border. Has Scotland *qua* Scotland ever been so influential in the world? There's so much turning on what her sons and daughters do on Thursday.

## Sunday 15 September 2014

Final straight. Race too close to call. John Curtice's poll-of-polls puts in at 51% No; 49% Yes.[157]

The flurry of weekend polls looks like this:

Survation/Better Together: 54% no; 46% yes.
ICM/*Guardian*: 51% no; 49% yes.
ICM/*Sunday Telegraph*: 54% yes; 46% no.
Panelbase/*Sunday Times*: 50.6% No; 49.4% Yes.

The ICM/Sun Tel is based on only 750 people, about three-quarters of the usual poll.

What have I picked up on the Whitehall front this week apart from the 'near panic' I've already reported?

That it was 'totally and utterly' a mistake not to make contingency plans. But the Cabinet formally reiterated that there shall be none when it met two weeks ago. Apparently the PM was very firm (I suspect word had reached him that little bits of informal work had been going on – 'the contingency plan that isn't a contingency plan', as it was put to me).

Naturally, thought is being given to the immediate consequences of a Yes. Parliament, both Houses, will have to be recalled. Party Conferences cancelled?

Papers dripping with anticipation today about David Cameron's fate if it's a Yes. Looks like plenty more than the 46 signatures needed on a letter to the chairman of the 1922 Committee to trigger a vote on his leadership. John Redwood is taking the lead on the English Question if it's devo-max: 'England cannot accept a position where Scotland fixes her own income tax and also sends MPs to

Westminster to help set an income tax rate for England too.'[158]

I find any degree of detachment is impossible on the fate of the kingdom. Sunday thoughts are quite natural about tough weeks to come; a bit of psychological preparation for the worst. But I've never faced anything quite like this because there hasn't been anything like this in the days, months, years and decades I have been breathing since 28 March, 1947. God knows if I'll be able to keep as cool as I should be on the BBC results programme and *Today* if it's a Yes. Perhaps I shouldn't even try to.

If the UK is severed on Thursday, in my mind thereafter, every day until I draw my last breath, there will be an elegy playing for a lost union; for a Scotland departed. It's as simple as that.

### Monday 15 September 2014

The Queen produced what history will record as her 'Crathie moment' after church yesterday near Balmoral. The police allowed photographers and reporters to get close as she chatted to well-wishers (not usually the case). Someone joked that they were not going to mention the referendum to which she replied:

You have an important vote on Thursday.

HMQ went on to say:

Well I hope people will think very carefully about the future.[159]

Neutral – but nicely and very neatly done.

*The Times* carries a terrific picture of HMQ and a kilted Prince Philip smiling as she approaches the crowd with Lady Sue Hussey and a detective a few feet behind.

In the campaign both Salmond and Darling made plain that Thursday is it – not like a general election where you can change your mind next time (Darling) while Salmond said: 'This is a once-in-a-generation, perhaps a once-in-a-lifetime, opportunity for Scotland.' Salmond added that if it's a Yes he'll start negotiating break-up pretty well straight away.[160]

Jim Naughtie was interesting on *Today* this morning. He said neither camp knew what will happen despite their public utterances – but there may be a tide surging in one direction or another under the surface that the polls have not picked up.

This ties in with what Tam Dalyell was saying on the phone yesterday. Local Labour friends and Tam's son Gordon have noticed voters in working-class districts 'saying quietly from behind closed doors "Of course we'll vote No."' Glasgow, Tam thought, is not quite the problem it's been portrayed: 'Dundee is the one ... It's going to be a tough week'. Tam was much amused when he heard that Dennis Skinner had been called a 'Red Tory' by a heckler in Midlothian.

### Tuesday 16 September 2014

David Cameron made the speech of his life in Aberdeen yesterday. Was home in time to watch it live on BBC News 24. As he warmed up, I scribbled 'real passion' and at the end 'best ever speech'.

On Friday we 'could be living in a different country with a different place in the world ... We are a family. Four nations in a single country. That can be difficult but it's wonderful ... Please, please don't let anyone tell you you can't be a proud Scot and a proud Brit ...Vote to save our United Kingdom'.

The BBC is leading this morning with a pledge in the *Daily Record* from Cameron, Miliband and Clegg on the permanence of the Scottish parliament and the Barnett formula. Will get details when I reach Westminster.

Here it is, under the headline 'THE VOW'.[161]

Some serious fumes swirl out of this.

Are the three leaders suggesting that we create a new type of statute – an entrenching Act, which no future Westminster Parliament can touch – to ensure that the Scotland Act 1998 cannot be repealed where it touches the existence of Holyrood?

Can you create a binding convention ensuring that a resource allocation mechanism – the Barnett formula – cannot be altered or abandoned? I think not.

The last two weeks has seen the devo-max option, which the Government prevented being placed as a third option on Thursday's ballot papers, making the running as the Union-preserving saviour of those who wish us to stay together. It is the visible, tangible evidence of panic and near desperation.

The PM's 'head and heart and soul, we want you to stay' speech,[162] has not protected him from sharp criticism for his lack of strategic thinking and planning and the way No.10 operates generally. Rachel Sylvester is blistering in today's *Times*:

> Complacency, cockiness and cliquiness: senior Tories fear that the Scottish referendum campaign has exposed the underlying flaws in the Downing Street operation that will become ever more pronounced as the general election nears. They point to a trademark tendency to put tactics before strategy that will also be a huge issue for the country and the Conservative party if a renegotiation and referendum on Europe ever go ahead.[163]

Whatever happens in two days time, the English question is going to roar into life.

Bernard Jenkin is on the case today with a letter in *The Times*. In a cluster under the headline 'How to address the West Lothian question', he writes:

Sir, You are right to endorse the answer to the West Lothian question ... proposed by John Redwood (who, contrary to your assertion, has often called big issues right, such as the disastrous European exchange rate mechanism).

The idea of 'English votes for English laws' was the basis for the 2010 Conservative manifesto commitment to set up what became the Mackay Commission in 2012. Devo-max makes implementation of its key principle even more urgent, namely that 'decisions at the United Kingdom level with a separate and distinct effect for England (or for England and Wales) should normally be taken only with the consent of a majority of MPs for constituencies in England (or England and Wales)'. This can be given effect by resolution of the House of Commons, rather than by legislation, and would give the English an effective parliament.

There would, however, be consequences for Whitehall. We could never have a Scottish UK chancellor setting English taxes in England at the annual budget but not in his or her own constituency. So Parliament will have to consider how to establish an English executive, with an English first minister and finance minister, along with England-only departments for matters such as health, education and local government, made accountable to English MPs alone.

This does not preclude enhanced functions for

counties and cities (rather than for artificial reasons), but that would be a matter for the new English executive.

Lunch with John Sewel, H of L Chairman of Committees and former Vice-Chancellor of the University of Aberdeen. John thinks both Houses of Parliament will need to be recalled on Monday even if it's a No vote as Alex Salmond won't hang about – he'll lay out in the Scottish Parliament (which will be sitting) all the things he expects Westminster and the London Government will need to do according to all the pledges made.

He reminds me of Sewel's Law: 'We like to say constitutional changes need to be made slowly and on the basis of consensus when we only ever make constitutional changes on the back of a crisis.'

Had a brief chat with Tina Stowell [Conservative leader of the House of Lords] this morning and urged upon her the desirability of not rushing if we stay together – of a declaratory White Paper with headings and not racing to a draft Bill by the end of January, as constitutions need careful construction if they are to endure and bring the stability and predictability which is their purpose.

### Wednesday 17 September 2014
Polls still on a razor-blade. Three of them put it on 52% No; 48% Yes.[164]

The nasty side of the clash of patriotisms came through yesterday. Ed Miliband couldn't get a hearing in the St James Shopping Centre in Edinburgh and had to evacuate the building.[165] George Galloway had been told he was going to 'face a bullet' during a meeting in Glasgow on Monday night.[166]

Alex Salmond has released an open letter to the Scottish people on this the final push day. Shrewd move.

The *Telegraph's* Opinium poll indicated No has a 16 point lead among women who have decided which way to vote.[167] If that holds, it will be the women of Scotland who save the Union tomorrow.

Magnus Linklater in *The Times* has an interview he recorded with David Cameron just before he went on stage in Aberdeen on Monday.

It's an Edith Piaf refrain: no regrets (e.g. about not having devo-max on the ballot paper). He acknowledges the prospect of defeat keeps him awake at night.[168] A Conservative MP, Andrew Rosindell, has come out about the PM's position after a Yes: 'the prime minister will have to decide what the honourable thing is to do', he told the *FT*.[169] To lose the United Kingdom on your watch would hole any premiership. But would it hole Cameron below the waterline? Would the aghast factor swing enough MPs to side with those who spend their waking hours wishing him out of No.10 for other reasons?

Still think we'll just be together at 7am on Friday morning.

Gordon Brown has found himself. By all account his speech in Clydebank yesterday was a *tour de force*.[170] According to the 'Londoner's Diary' in this afternoon's *Evening Standard*, David Cameron revealed at last night's party in No.10 to launch Andy Marr's novel *Head of State*, that he has been having regular chats with his predecessor: 'I've never had so many before. We're actually good friends.'[171]

Bump into Dafydd Wigley [Plaid Cymru peer] in the House of Commons cloisters on the way home:

PH: What do you reckon?
DW: I've just been up there. Too close to call. You can feel the surge in Glasgow and Dundee but you can't in Edinburgh and the Borders. The effects of a No are going to be considerable. There will be great acrimony if they don't get what they have been promised – getting it through down here [i.e. the Westminster Parliament].
PH: And the percussive effects will be considerable elsewhere. Wales will want Silk II [the plan for further devolution to Wales] – if not more. Then there's the English Question. It's Tommy Cooper-style constitution making – just like that.
DW: (Laughs). He'd have done a better job!

A whisper reached me yesterday afternoon that if it's a Yes, Parliament could well be recalled for a sitting on Saturday. It would, I think, be the first time since the Falklands.

### Thursday 18 September 2014
*Der Tag*. The Day.
The final flurry of polls sharpened the knife-edge.

| | |
|---|---|
| YouGov: | 52% No; 48% Yes |
| IPSOS MORI: | 51% No; 49% Yes |
| Panelbase: | 52% No; 48% Yes |
| Survation | 53% No; 47% Yes[172] |

Passions rose; some behaviour coarsened.[173]

Gordon Brown was magnificent again – his great fists beating like steam hammers during a speech in Maryhill, Glasgow. I reckon this was the speech of his life. He was aflame:

> Let no narrow nationalism split asunder what we have built together in Britain. Tell them this is our Scotland. Tell them that Scotland does not belong to the SNP. Scotland does not belong to the Yes campaign.
>
> Scotland does not belong to any politician ... Scotland belongs to all of us. This is not their flag, their country, their culture, their streets. This is everyone's flag, everyone's country, everyone's culture and everyone's streets. Let us tell the people of Scotland that we who vote No love Scotland.[174]

The ever well-informed Patrick Wintour has a story in *The Guardian* about Gordon Brown's plan to remake the British constitution if it's a No:

> Gordon Brown, in pole position in the event of a No vote to be hailed as the man who saved the union, has crafted a plan for a post-referendum constitutional settlement in the UK, including a new role for an elected House of Lords as an arbiter in disputes between the four nations.[175]

The GB idea is that the Lords be replaced by an elected senate representative of the regions and nations with powers to block legislation for two years if proposed legislation threatens the unity of the kingdom.

Alistair Carmichael has given *The Guardian* an interview in which he says if it's a narrow Yes and Shetland votes strongly No it could seek to stay part of the UK with a similar status to the Isle of Man. It's not entirely clear if Alistair is including Orkney in this.[176]

I'm writing this about 9.45am on Thursday. Strange to think that by this time tomorrow my country could have a very different political, economic *and* emotional roof over all our heads. Imagining what will have to happen over the next few days if it's Yes:

### Friday (Tomorrow)
*Won't know the result until the Glasgow and Edinburgh returns come in towards the end between 5 and 6am. Returning officers in the 32 districts can allow recounts. Suspect that when in doubt they will, which will delay matters.*

*PM and HM Queen. Surely he will want to go to Balmoral in person rather than phone from Downing Street. So swift flight from Northolt to Aberdeen to Balmoral and back. You can't tell the Sovereign you've lost her kingdom by telephone. Announcement that both House of Parliament will be recalled – probably for Monday.*

*Treasury and Bank of England (which does have a contingency plan) will be active from the moment the markets open.*

*Cabinet meets on Friday afternoon.*

We will be, as a wise insider friend puts it, 'in completely uncharted territory'. *The Cabinet Manual* is silent on how to dismember the kingdom.

Other possibilities? Labour Party Conference due to start over the weekend cancelled? Certainly all the parliamentary parties will have to meet.

Waking up following an afternoon to get some sleep in the bank (no more kip until I'm on the train to Sheffield tomorrow afternoon) all this seems so distant and unreal – yet it's possible.

*For entries for Friday 19 September and Saturday 20 September see 'The Result' on pages 13–24.*

## Monday 22 September 2014

A number of chats today with officials, ex-officials and politicos. Two mutually reinforcing streams of thought.

(a) It's all a terrible, un-thought-out mess
(b) Party and personal politics has resumed with a vengeance, with the parties and the party leaders trying to squeeze maximum advantage out of the Scottish Question (in its new form) and the English Question (in its waking form) with Alex Salmond sneering at the lot of them as a bunch of shameless renegers.

Saw the glorious Maurice Saatchi at Westminster Abbey this evening. 'It's all a mess and it's all your fault', he said by way of greeting. 'What are you going to do to solve it? Haven't you got a plan?'

What we need are a set of arrangements that will:

(a) allow a mutual flourishing (a Justin Welby phrase about the wings of the Church of England) in the constituent nations of the UK and within those nations

(b) help us find a way of doing things together as a union.

Discussed all this at the British Academy's Strategic Advisory Committee this afternoon. Mary Beard and I suggested the Academy prepare a primer on the options, how each relates to the others and containing a series of tests to apply to the competing solutions.

Time for the political class to raise its game. Not the slightest sign of that yet.

### Tuesday 23 September 2014

The English Question will form part of the contest in the May 2015 general election. That was the message from the Chequers meeting yesterday between the PM and his backbenchers.[177] William Hague, who is to chair the new Cabinet Committee, said so, publicly warning Ed Miliband he would suffer at the ballot box if he blocks English home rule: 'If other parties make it impossible to deal with this issue in tandem, then it will be an issue at the general election in May ...'[178] But Hague also made it plain the promises to Scotland would be honoured even if the opposition stymied plans for more devolution to England.[179]

Spoke to a still palpably relieved but rather weary Whitehall insider who said 'There are two big parts to the constitutional stuff':

1: 'The Vow' and devo-max. It's going to be a

> nightmare in terms of time but we can probably
> do that.
>
> 2: The second, which is totally undoable, is the English
> stuff. There's no political agreement whatever.
> William Hague is trying to marry the two.[180]

The PM is in New York for the UN General Assembly. A directional microphone picks him up walking and talking down a corridor. When he rang the Queen on Friday morning to say 'It's all right. It's okay', she 'purred down the line', according to David Cameron. 'But it should never have been that close. It wasn't in the end.'[181]

Paddy Ashdown (with whom I share a mutual pleasure in winding each other up on House of Lords reform) hails me from the end of the West Side corridor:

> PA: The House of Lords may well be a goner. The constitutional convention will put that right.
> PH: I knew you were going to say that.

The world's – and the UK's – attention is moving away from Scotland. The US launched Tomahawk and air strikes on ISIS in Syria last night. Parliament may be recalled on Friday to approve RAF participation – whether in Syria as well as Iraq isn't clear.

### Wednesday 24 September 2014

This morning's papers, naturally, have a fuller account of what David Cameron said about Scotland and HM Queen to Michael Bloomberg, the former Mayor of New York, yesterday:

The definition of relief is being the prime minister of the United Kingdom and ringing the Queen and saying: 'It's alright, it's OK.' That was something. She purred down the line ... But it should never have been that close. It wasn't close in the end, but there was a time in the middle of the campaign when it felt ...

I've said I want to find these polling companies and I want to sue them for my stomach ulcers because of what they put me through. It was very nervous moments.[182]

The *Telegraph* reports that the BBC enhanced the sound still further and claim the PM added: 'I've never heard someone tear up like that. It was great.' Channel 4 News think it was 'cheer up'.[183]

The new Devolution Cabinet Committee meets for the first time today.* It promises to be a leaky one. The Lib Dems have got in first. *The Guardian* is reporting that: 'Danny Alexander, the most senior Scottish member of the Cabinet, is expected to "read the riot act" over confusing Tory messages which allowed Salmond to claim that Cameron was reneging on his pledge to devolve further powers to the Scottish parliament.'[184] These boys give the impression of squabbling labourers rather than the Masterbuilders on a new constitutional construction site.

---

* It's formally known as the Ministerial Committee on Devolution and its membership is: William Hague (Chair); Danny Alexander (Deputy Chair); George Osborne; Iain Duncan-Smith; Eric Pickles; Alistair Carmichael; Stephen Crabbe; Oliver Letwin; David Laws; Michael Gove; Tina Stowell; Jim Wallace; Don Foster; Greg Clark.

## Thursday 25 September 2014

Seven days in September. A week ago the Prime Minister – and plenty others – was in a state of anxiety about the rupture of the kingdom. Today he's preparing his Cabinet to take us to war in the Middle East, provided the House of Commons backs him tomorrow on airstrikes against ISIS in Iraq. All this and he's brimming with remorse after inadvertently placing the Queen's inner thoughts about the Scottish outcome for ever in the ether and the eternal record. *The Times* reports this morning that No.10 has already been in touch with the Palace to convey his regret and that he will apologise in person at his next audience.[185]

What a time the Queen has had, from her Crathie Moment to what we can now call the Relief of Balmoral. Both of them deserve to become the subject of a grand oil painting along the lines of Landseer's 'The Monarch of the Glen'. Was with part of the intelligence community today. Suggested that the capturing of David Cameron's conversation with Michael Bloomberg was rather like a rare and spectacular SIGINT breakthrough at GCHQ for those interested in observing that most secret and sensitive relationship between the Head of State and Head of Government. There was, naturally, a certain amount of shared relief swilling around. One droll Intell veteran said: 'If they'd won, it would have been President Salmond in five years.' This is *not* a judgement based on any assessment by British Intelligence. They, too, were banned from contingency planning of any kind – and the future of the Monarchy in Scotland would not have been any part of their horizon-scanning had it been permitted.

Most of the insiders I've talked to this week think that the 'no contingency planning' diktat was 'high risk', as one of them put it. Whitehall is certainly going to have to make up for it now if the Gordon Brown timetable – accepted by the other party leaders – is to be fulfilled. It is:

**End of October 2014:** Publication of a Command Paper setting out all the proposals for the new powers to be devolved to Scotland followed by consultation.

**End of November 2014:** Publication of a White Paper setting out the powers proposed for transfer.

**25 January 2015 (Burns' Night):** Draft law to be published ahead of a House of Commons vote.

**Easter 2015:** Gordon Brown has said he would like the Bill to have had its second reading by Easter.

**7 May 2015:** General Election.

**June 2015:** Brown has said he wants to see the Bill brought in by the end of the first legislative week of the new Parliament.

For all the rebirth of Gordon Brown, it is up to Parliament and not him to determine the ticking of the clock. It would, for example, be folly not to have proper pre-legislative scrutiny of any proposed Bill by a Joint Committee of both Houses of Parliament. GB plainly thinks that can be accommodated within such a timetable.

Such a rush might suit the metabolic rate of politics in Scotland, still racing after two years of independence debate (look at the surge in SNP membership to over 50,000 this last week[186]). England's appetite for devo-max is, to put it mildly, torpid compared to north of the border. The English Question is the weathermaker now and it will continue to be influential even as the political low pressure systems come squalling in as they do, one after another, as we get closer to a general election. We'll need to wait for that end-of-October Command Paper before we have any real idea of the kingdom to come.

# Epilogue

# Maps in the mind

In the first weeks of 2015, political thoughts naturally became more and more directed towards the May general election. Elections are mood-makers and mind-concentrators by their very nature. Once the draft clauses of the future Scotland Bill and the Conservative proposals for English Votes for English Laws were published, the Kingdom to come was afforded little or no attention by the politicians or the press.

It remained, however, a first-order question of strategic proportions for the UK. The great American commentator, Walter Lippmann, argued that public opinion is an accumulation of the pictures individuals carry in their heads.[187] Will there be a union-sized and UK-shaped map in the minds of the young men and women who will stream into the Scottish electorate in time, say, for a referendum in the early 2020s, by which time the older, more naturally unionist cohorts who voted in 2014 will have either left the sacred turf and moor of Scotland or be getting close to their final departures? Will the Union be part of the coming generation's spirit of place? Will the purposes of remaining together bite into their consciousness or their expectations?

As I penned these last paragraphs I talked to a seasoned figure very close in to the 2014 referendum and its aftermath. I asked him what odds he would give on the Union being intact in 20 years. 'Fifty-fifty', he replied without hesitation.

We went through the factors that bind in the UK. We came up with a list that help us think and behave as a Union:

- The Queen
- The Armed Forces
- The welfare state/National Health Service
- Economic stability
- The BBC
- The UK passport
- The Olympic Games (every four years)

Potent though those factors are, we need more – considerably more. The Union is no longer a fixed map in the collective UK mind; no longer an automatic pilot guiding shared consciousness. I wish it were. I profoundly hope it can be once more.

# Notes

1   Winston.S.Churchill, *The World Crisis 1911–1915*, (Thornton Butterworth, 1923), pp.212–13.

2   Cited in D.R. Thorpe, *Eden: The Life and Times of Anthony Eden First Earl of Avon, 1897–1977*, (Chatto and Windus, 2003), p.3.

3   Peter Laslett, *The World We Have Lost*.

4   Keith Middlemas, *Power, Competition and the State Vol 1: Britain in Search of Balance 1940–61*, (Macmillan, 1988), p.116.

5   *Social Insurance and Allied Services. Report by Sir William Beveridge*, Cmd 6404 (HMSO, 1942).

6   Charles de Gaulle, *War Memoirs Volume One, The Call to Honour 1940–1942*, (Collins, 1955), p.9.

7   George Orwell, *The Lion and the Unicorn: Socialism and the English Genius*, (first published by Secker and Warburg, 1941), most easily consulted in Peter Davison (ed), *Orwell's England*, (Penguin, 2001), pp.250–76.

8   Ibid, p.251.

9   Ibid, p.264.

10  David Runciman, *The Confidence Trap: A History of Democracy in Crisis from World War I to the Present*, (Princeton University Press, 2013), pp.1–34, 264–93.

11  Andrew Whitaker, 'Great and good sign up to urge Scots to vote No', *The Scotsman*, 8 August 2014.

12    'Independence question. The vote in full', *The Times*, 20
      September 2014.

13    Sam Coates, Lindsay McIntosh, 'Wipeout for Labour
      looms in Scotland', *The Times*, 31 October 2014.

14    Daniel Boffey, 'Miliband in new crisis as senior MPs
      back leadership change', *The Observer*, 9 November
      2014.

15    Lindsay McIntosh, Sam Coates, 'Most Scots now
      support separation from the Union', *The Times*, 1
      November 2014.

16    House of Lords, *Official Report*, 29 October 2014,
      col.1216.

17    Private information.

18    House of Lords, *Official Report*, 29 October 2014,
      col.1216.

19    Ibid, cols.1296–97.

20    Ibid, col.1296.

21    Ibid, col.1235.

22    Ibid, cols, 1234–35.

23    Ibid, col.1219.

24    Ibid, col.1297.

25    'Labour announces plans to give regions and nations
      greater power and a stronger voice in Westminster',
      http://press.labour.org.uk/post/101667859054/
      labour-announces-plans-to-give-regions.

26    'Elected senate would replace House of Lords
      under Labour', http://www.bbc.co.uk/news/
      uk-politics-29857849, 1 November 2014.

27    *The Smith Commission: Report of the Smith Commission
      for further devolution of powers to the Scottish*

*Parliament*. (Smith Commission, Edinburgh, 27 November 2014).

28  *The Implications of Devolution for England*, Cm 8969, (Stationery Office, 16 December 2014).

29  *The Smith Commission*, p.3.

30  Ibid, p.5.

31  Ibid, p.6.

32  Ibid, p.12.

33  Ibid.

34  Ibid, p.13

35  Lord Hope of Craighead, *The Kingdom to Come*, BBC Radio 4, 16 December 2014.

36  *The Smith Commission*, p.15.

37  Ibid, p.16.

38  Ibid, p.21.

39  Ibid, pp.18–19.

40  Ibid, p.23.

41  Ibid.

42  Ibid, pp.26–27.

43  Ibid, p.27.

44  Alistair Darling, *The Kingdom to Come*, BBC Radio 4, 18 December 2014.

45  Ibid.

46  Ibid.

47  William Hague, *The Kingdom to Come*, BBC Radio 4, 19 December 2014.

48  *The Implications for Devolution for England*, Cm 8969, chapter six, pp.22–32.

49  Ibid, p.28.

50  Ibid, pp.25–27.

51 Rt Hon. William Hague MP, 'Speech to launch Conservative Party EVEL proposal', 3 February 2015.

52 House of Commons, *Official Report*, 4 February 2015, col 391.

53 Ibid, col. 396.

54 Nicola Sturgeon, 'Commentary', *Observer*, 8 February 2015.

55 Conversation with Dominic Grieve, 30 January 2015.

56 I am grateful to Douglas Hurd for this metaphor. In conversation on 27 January 2015, Lord Hurd said people wished to feel at ease with the 'political roof over their heads'.

57 *The Implications for Devolution for England*, Cm 8969, chapter six, p.27.

58 William Hague, *The Kingdom to Come*.

59 Tom Clark and Severin Carrell, 'Labour faces Scotland bloodbath', *The Guardian*, 27 December 2014.

60 Ibid.

61 'What the polls tells us. Colour of the country 2010 and 2015', *The Guardian*, 27 December 2014.

62 For Parnell see G.R.Searle, *A New England? Peace and War 1886–1918*, (OUP, 2004), pp.141, 157–8; John Cannon (ed), *The Oxford Companion to British History*, (OUP, 1997), pp.731–2.

63 Nigel Morris, 'Salmond hints at Scottish votes for English laws', *The Independent*, 19 December 2014.

64 *Scotland in the United Kingdom: An enduring settlement* Cm 8990, (Stationery Office, 22 January 2015).

65 Lindsay McIntosh, 'SNP "trying to wreck" devolution deal', *The Times*, 23 January 2015.

66 Sam Coates, Francis Elliott, Lindsay McIntosh, 'SNP to vote on English laws. Nationalists gear up to hold balance of power as poll points to Labour wipe out in Scotland', *The Times*, 22 January 2015.

67 Private information.

68 House of Lords, *Official Report*, 22 January 2015, col.1490.

69 Baroness O'Neill of Bengarve, *The Kingdom to Come*, BBC Radio 4, 17 December 2014.

70 Lord Butler of Brockwell, *The Kingdom to Come*, BBC Radio 4, 15 December 2014.

71 Lord Hope of Craighead, *The Kingdom to Come*.

72 House of Commons Political and Constitutional Reform Committee, *A new Magna Carta?* Second Report of Session 2014–15, HC 463 (Stationery Office, July 2014).

73 Lord Neuberger, 'The UK Constitutional Settlement and the Role of the UK Supreme Court', Legal Wales Conference, Bangor, 10 October 2014.

74 Ibid.

75 'David Cameron: Speech to the Conservative Party Conference 2014', (Conservative Party, 1 October 2014)

76 Lord Neuberger, 'The UK Constitutional Settlement and the Role of the UK Supreme Court'.

77 The phrase 'tacit understandings' is Sir Sidney Low's. See his *The Governance of England*, (Fisher Unwin, 1904), p.12.

78 House of Commons Political and Constitutional Reform Committee, 'Revisiting the Cabinet Manual', Sir Jeremy Heywood, Secretary of the Cabinet, oral evidence, 17 July 2014, Qu.121; Matt Ross, 'The Delivery Men', *Civil Service World*, July 2014, p.36.

79 Private information.

80 Private information.

81 Kevin Schofield, 'We're Scot to say "No"', *The Sun*, 11 August 2014.

82 'Scottish independence: Alistair Carmichael pledges devolution talks', BBC News Scotland Politics, 21 May 2014, http://www.bbc.co.uk/news/uk-scotland-scotland-politics-27500213.

83 Simon Jenkins, 'Trident is absurd. Scotland may help us get rid of it', *The Guardian*, 15 August 2014.

84 TNS press release, 13 August 2014.

85 John Redwood, 'Freedom and England', The 2014 McWhirter Memorial Lecture, The Freedom Association, 13 August 2014.

86 Kate Devlin, 'Call to ban Scots from taking health and education roles', *The Herald*, 14 August 2014.

87 Kevin McKenna, 'Scotland's leading historian makes up his mind: it's yes to independence', *The Observer*, 17 August 2014.

88 Tim Montgomerie, 'Those who want the UK to split are not the friends of freedom', *The Times*, 16 August 2014.

89 Magnus Magnusson, *Scotland*, pp.188–89.

90 'Comparing Scotland's campaigns. Aye'll be back', *The Economist*, 16 August 2014.

91  Lindsay McIntosh, Sam Coates, 'Pollsters claim real shift in opinion as "Yes" vote rises', *The Times*, 18 August 2014.

92  Valentine Low, Hamish Macdonell, 'Independent Scotland could lose royal family', *The Times*, 18 August 2014.

93  Nicholas Watt and Libby Brooks, 'PM rejects Salmond claim over health service in Scotland', *The Guardian*, 19 August 2014.

94  Chris Green, 'Salmond cannot keep the pound, says Alexander', *The Independent*, 19 August 2014.

95  Ibid.

96  Polly Toynbee, 'Shared values matter more than where the border lies', *The Guardian*, 19 August 2014.

97  Deborah Haynes, Lindsay McIntosh, Hamish Macdonell, 'Independent Scotland has no guarantee of a place in Nato', *The Times*, 19 August 2014.

98  Ibid.

99  Chris Green, 'Most English people want Scotland to stay, as long as things change', *The Independent*, 20 August 2014.

100  Wales Governance Centre, 'The English favour a hard line with Scotland – whatever the result of the Independence Referendum', http://sites.cardiff.ac.uk/wgc/2014/08/20/the-english-favour-a-hard-line-with-Scotland.

101  Tim Montgomerie, 'Scots beware: the English backlash is about to begin', *The Times*, 20 August 2014.

102  Lindsay McIntosh, 'Salmond's oil sums "do not add up"', *The Times*, 21 August 2014.

103  Chris Green, 'Scotland "overestimates" North Sea oil', *The Independent on Sunday*, 24 August 2014.

104  Ibid.

105  Severin Carrell and Libby Brooks, 'All to play for, says Yes campaign, with eye on crucial don't knows', *The Guardian*, 23 August 2014.

106  Hamish Macdonell, 'Salmond puts focus on health for final debate', *The Times*, 25 August 2014.

107  Michael Savage, 'Cameron ready to threaten withdrawal from Brussels', *The Times*, 25 August 2014.

108  Severin Carrell and Libby Brooks, 'Salmond emerges on top in tough TV debate', *The Guardian*, 26 August 2014.

109  Conversation with Tam Dalyell, 26 August 2014.

110  Michael White, 'Lofty talk and a lot of arm-waving', *The Guardian*, 26 August 2014.

111  The letter was published in *The Scotsman,* 27 August 2014.

112  The letter was published in *The Herald*, 28 August 2014.

113  Peter Sutherland, 'Brexit is in Scot's hands', *The Guardian*, 28 August 2014.

114  Nicholas Watt, Libby Brooks, Simon Goodley, 'Cameron in plea to Scots on UK trade', *The Guardian*, 28 August 2014.

115  Sam Coates, Laura Pitel, 'Cameron braced for more UKIP defections', *The Times*, 29 August 2014.

116  Mike Wade, 'Egg attack on MP leaves nasty taste', *The Times*, 29 August 2014.

117  Ibid.

118 Libby Brooks, 'Cameron met with Yes camp heckles and humour as he tries to avoid the protestors,' *The Guardian*, 29 August 2014.

119 Mike Wade, 'Yes campaign must call off the mobs, says MP after egg attack', *The Times*, 30 August 2014.

120 Lindsay McIntosh, Hamish Macdonell, 'McCartney in storm of abuse after urging Scotland to stay', *The Times*, 1 September 2014.

121 Magnus Linklater, 'In a dark corner of Scots nationalism intolerance lurks', *The Times*, 1 September 2014.

122 http://blog.whatscotlandthinks.org/2014/08/yes-bounce-back-in-survation-post-bbc-debate-poll.

123 http://blog.whatscotlandthinks.org/2014/08/poll-of-polls-28-august/

124 Lindsay McIntosh, Sam Coates, 'Scotland poll puts Union on knife edge. Independence campaign three points from victory', *The Times*, 2 September 2014.

125 Magnus Linklater, 'Now at last the No camp realise the fight is on', *The Times*, 2 September 2014.

126 George Parker, Delphine Strauss, Sarah O'Connor, 'Scots vote fears rattle City', *Financial Times*, 3 September 2014.

127 Francis Elliott, Lindsay McIntosh, Sam Coates, 'Shock poll forces the Treasury to prepare for independence turmoil', *The Times*, 3 September 2014.

128 Severin Carrell, Katie Allen, Libby Brooks, 'Scotland could not joint EU without deal on the pound, says currency expert', *The Guardian*, 3 September 2014.

129  Lindsay McIntosh, 'Fear of bitter aftermath, whatever the outcome', *The Times*, 3 September 2014.

130  Mike Wade, 'Murphy returns to campaign and shows he's no chicken', *The Times*, 3 September 2014.

131  'Scots vote fears rattle City', *Financial Times*, 3 September 2014.

132  James Titcomb, 'Yes vote could cause sterling crash', *Daily Telegraph*, 4 September 2014.

133  Nicholas Watt and Severin Carrell, 'PM urged to delay 2015 election if Scotland says yes to independence', *The Guardian*, 4 September 2014.

134  Chris Green, '"Just Tories in Red Ties": Miliband's attempt to rally the union falls flat', *The Independent*, 4 September 2014.

135  James Cusick, 'Rebel MPs plot instant revolt against Cameron if Yes campaign win', *The Independent*, 4 September 2014.

136  John Scarlett, 'A Yes vote brings grave security dangers', *The Times*, 5 September 2014.

137  Tim Shipman and Jason Allardyce, 'Yes leads in Scots poll shock', *The Sunday Times*, 7 September 2014. See also Martin Arnold, Steven Foley, Jonathan Guthrie and Charles Parker, 'Scots vote fears rattle investors', *Financial Times*, 7 September 2014; Severin Carrell and Patrick Wintour, 'Brown to the rescue? No camp sends for ex-PM to save union', *The Guardian*, 7 September 2014.

138  Hamish Macdonell, Francis Elliott, 'Parties unite in last-ditch bid to save the union', *The Times*, 8 September 2014.

139  Philip Aldrick, 'Poll swing will push down the pound', *The Times*, 8 September 2014.

140  http://blog.whatscotlandthinks.org/2014/09/maybe-yes-maybe-no-new-yougov-and-panelbase-polls/.

141  Martin Kettle, 'Analysis. Nothing else matters in British politics', *The Guardian*, 8 September 2014.

142  Hamish Macdonell, '"Yes" voters don't want the Queen', *The Times*, 8 September 2014.

143  Gordon Rayner, Christopher Hope and Peter Dominiczak, 'Scottish Independence. The Queen is urged to intervene', *The Daily Telegraph*, 9 September 2014.

144  Sam Coates, Lindsay McIntosh, Valentine Low, 'Don't drag me into this debate, says the Queen', *The Times*, 10 September 2014.

145  'UK RIP?', *The Economist*, September 13th-19th 2014.

146  Sam Coates, Lindsay McIntosh, 'Support for independent Scotland on the slide', *The Times*, 12 September 2014.

147  Sarah Gordon, Patrick Jenkins, Martin Arnold, George Parker and Sam Fleming, 'Scots warned on decade of uncertainty', *Financial Times*, 12 September 2014.

148  Alan Cochrane, 'Cheery chappy Alex shows his sour side as pressure builds', *The Daily Telegraph*, 12 September 2014.

149  Sarah Neville and Clive Cookson, 'Ruling elite aghast as union wobbles', *Financial Times*, 12 September 2014.

150  Tom Clark, Severin Carrell, Nick Watt, Jill Treanor, 'Union hanging by a thread as yes campaign narrows gap', *The Guardian*, 13 September 2014.

151   Harry Wilson, Philip Aldrick, Sam Coates, 'Investors dump £17bn amid fears over union', *The Times*, 13 September 2014.

152   Simon Johnson and Matthew Holehouse, 'Money floods out of UK over Yes vote fears', *The Daily Telegraph*, 13 September 2014.

153   Ben Farmer, 'Yes will be a body blow to Forces, warn Navy chiefs', *The Daily Telegraph*, 13 September 2014.

154   'Investors dump £17bn...' *The Times*, 14 September 2014.

155   Simon Johnson, 'We'll get revenge on businesses that threaten to leave, says Salmond ally', *The Daily Telegraph*, 14 September 2014.

156   Robin Harding, 'IMF warns on secession risk in markets', *Financial Times*, 13 September 2014.

157   BBC Radio 4 7am news, 15 September 2014.

158   Tim Shipman, Jason Allardyce, 'Cameron: split will be forever', *The Sunday Times*, 14 September 2014.

159   Simon Johnson, Ausian Cramb, Christopher Hope and Gordon Rayner, 'Queen breaks her silence over Scottish independence', *The Daily Telegraph*, 15 September 2014.

160   Hamish Macdonell, 'If we win by one vote the break-up will start the next day', *The Times*, 15 September 2014.

161   'The Vow', *Daily Record*, 16 September 2014.

162   Peter Dominiczak and Simon Johnson, 'PM begs Scots not leave the UK', *The Daily Telegraph*, 16 September 2014.

163   Rachel Sylvester, 'Cocky Cameron surrenders keys to the kingdom', *The Times*, 16 September 2014.

164  Magnus Linklater, Matt Dathan, Sam Coates, Francis Elliott, 'No regrets, says Cameron as MPs warn of rebellion', *The Times*, 17 September 2014.

165  Francis Elliott, Lindsay McIntosh, 'Campaign chaos as Miliband is jostled by jeering Yes activists', *The Times*, 17 September 2014.

166  Chris Green, James Cusick and Nigel Morris, 'A nation divided against itself', *The Independent*, 17 September 2014.

167  Tim Ross, 'Women give No campaign the edge', *The Daily Telegraph*, 17 September 2014.

168  Magnus Linklater, 'Fear that makes Cameron wake up in a cold sweat', *The Times*, 17 September 2014.

169  Elizabeth Rigby, 'PM heads for backbench showdown', *Financial Times*, 17 September 2014.

170  Ben Riley-Smith, 'Tell your grandchildren what we achieved together, urges Brown', *The Daily Telegraph*, 17 September 2014.

171  Londoner's Diary'; 'A friend at last for Cameron in Scotland...' *London Evening Standard*, 17 September 2014.

172  Sam Coates, Lindsay McIntosh, 'Scotland decides', *The Times*, 18 September 2014.

173  Hamish Macdonell, Lindsay McIntosh, 'Waterbombs and insults fly as the rival campaigns clash', *The Times*, 18 September 2014.

174  Ben Riley-Smith, 'Stand and be counted, Brown tells Unionists', *The Daily Telegraph*, 18 September 2014.

175  Patrick Wintour, 'Brown could be the one to redesign UK if vote is no', *The Guardian*, 18 September 2014.

176  Esther Addley, 'Shetland may go it alone if rest of country votes yes, warns minister', *The Guardian*, 18 September 2014.

177  Holly Watt and Steven Swinford, 'English home rule at the heart of Tory campaign', *The Daily Telegraph*, 23 September 2014.

178  Nicholas Watt, 'Hague throws down general election gauntlet to Labour over devolution', *The Guardian*, 23 September 2014.

179  Scott Macnab, 'Hague says pledges to Scotland will be honoured', *The Scotsman*, 23 September 2014.

180  Private information.

181  BBC 1, *Six o'clock News*, 23 September 2014.

182  Rowena Mason, 'Cameron: Scotland result made Queen "purr down the line"', *The Guardian*, 24 September 2014.

183  Peter Dominiczak, 'Cameron says Queen "purred" at Scotland result', *The Daily Telegraph*, 24 September 2014.

184  Libby Brooks, Nicholas Watt, 'Salmond says voting age should be lowered to 16 for UK elections', *The Guardian*, 24 September 2014.

185  Michael Savage, 'Cameron apologises for saying Queen purred after "No" vote', *The Times*, 25 September 2014.

186  Jane Bradley, 'Yes voters flock to sign up for party politics', *The Scotsman*, 23 September 2014.

187  Walter Lippmann, *Public Opinion*, (Harcourt Brace, 1922).

# By the same Author

States of Emergency
(with Keith Jeffery)

Sources Close to the Prime Minister
(with Michael Cockerell and David Walker)

What the Papers Never Said

Cabinet

Ruling Performance
(edited with Anthony Seldon)

Whitehall

Never Again: Britain 1945–51

The Hidden Wiring: Unearthing the British Constitution

Muddling Through: Power, Politics and the Quality of
Government in Postwar Britain

The Prime Minister: The Office and Its Holders since 1945

The Secret State: Whitehall and the Cold War

Having It So Good: Britain in the Fifties

The New Protective State: Government, Intelligence and
Terrorism (editor)

Cabinets and the Bomb

The Secret State: Preparing for the Worst, 1945–2010

Distilling the Frenzy:
Writing the History of One's Own Times

Establishment and Meritocracy